Moving beyond capitalist agriculture

Could agroecology prevent further pandemics?

PANDEMIC RESEARCH FOR THE PEOPLE PReP

Published by
Daraja Press
https://darajapress.com

© 2021 Pandemic Research for the People

Cover image: Creative Market: Julia Dreams
Cover design and typesetting: Kate McDonnell

ISBN 9781988832975

Thinking Freedom Series editor: Firoze Manji
Moving Beyond Capitalism – Now! Series editor: Howard Waitzkin

Library and Archives Canada Cataloguing in Publication

Title: Moving beyond capitalist agriculture : could agroecology prevent further
    pandemics? / Pandemic Research for the People.
Names: Container of (work): Wallace, Robert G. Globalized food systems, structural
    inequality, and COVID-19. | Container of (work): Liebman, Alexander. Can
    agroecology stop COVID-21, -22, and -23? Moving beyond capitalist agriculture. |
    Pandemic Research for the People, author, publisher.
Description: Series statement: Moving beyond capitalism/Thinking freedom | Includes
    bibliographical references.
Identifiers: Canadiana (print) 20210233427 | Canadiana (ebook) 20210233850 | ISBN
    9781988832975   (softcover) | ISBN 9781988832982 (ebook)
Subjects: LCSH: Agricultural ecology. | LCSH: Agricultural ecology—Health aspects. |
    LCSH: Zoonoses—   Prevention.
Classification: LCC S589.7 .M68 2021 | DDC 577.5/5—dc23

Moving Beyond Capitalist Agriculture is born out of the coordination between scholars and community organizers and it should be shared widely. The group behind it, the Pandemic Research for the People, is an expression of collective wisdom and necessary unease. In fact, organization and solidarity are two values to be cherished in this moment of multiple crises. COVID-19 is a neoliberal disease and agroecology that frees the land and people of greed and towards food sovereignty is the pathway out of this mess.

> – **Saulo Araujo**, US Friends of the
> Landless Workers Movement

If you want to know more about the connections between racial capitalism, industrial agriculture, environmental destruction, and epidemics and pandemics, then this is a great place to start. But this pamphlet is more than just an analysis of the immense problems generated by capitalism. More importantly, this pamphlet represents an attempt to overcome this system and to develop revolutionary alternatives to it. Rather than falling into the tempting illusion of reform, the authors of these texts give invaluable insights into how we might support and develop revolutionary forms of agro-ecology that can sustain and reproduce life outside of the racial capitalist machine that is destroying it."

> – **Arturo Castillon**, co-author,
> *The Revolutionary Meaning of the*
> *George Floyd Uprising*

Increasingly threatening climate disaster coinciding with a pandemic has tragically illustrated that the world doesn't have the luxury of dealing with one crisis at a time - and capitalist agriculture is at the root of both.

The authors show convincingly that there is a better way: one that's based on self-determination and building on human cooperation, not competition. This publication makes a strong case for agroecology as a crucial part of a future that puts people above profit; a future that assures people`s health by allowing planetary health to flourish.

It will bring clarity to everyone trying to understand how the next pandemic could be averted whilst building a more just world

> – **Vijoleta Gordeljević**,
> Health economist and environmental
> health policy expert,
> People's Health Movement.

Table of Contents

Introductory note

Howard Waitzkin

Pandemic Research for the People (PReP) is doing some of the world's most important work in understanding and responding to the COVID-19 pandemic, as well as helping to prevent similar and even worse pandemics in the future.

With participants spanning multiple countries, PReP has become an interdisciplinary network of farmers, scientists in biology and the social sciences, and revolutionary activists. People in PReP collaborate with a common motivation to move beyond capitalist, industrial, racist agriculture. This destructive approach to agriculture, which arose fairly recently in human history, they identify as the main cause of dangerous, "zoonotic" infections that move from animals to human populations. Such unsafe conditions arise mainly due to destruction of forest habitats that previously buffered emerging infectious diseases so they did not spread, and due to the industrial production of meat, which fosters the emergence of ever more dangerous pathogens that cause life-threatening infections in humans and other animal species.

To move beyond the agriculture of racial capitalism, PReP is fostering an "agroecological" transformation to safer, less exploitative, more sustainable, and more enjoyable ways to produce food. These creative practices allow ecologically based food production not based on exploitation, racism, and capital accumulation. Agroecology also fosters the restoration of natural habitats that help prevent emerging pandemics.

During the COVID-19 pandemic, PReP has produced a sequence of "dispatches" that focus on the pandemic's causes, communities' creative responses, and agricultural innovations that help prevent future pandemics by moving beyond agricultural practices rooted in racial capitalism. This manifesto/pamphlet, which is part of the series on "Moving Beyond Capitalism – Now!", contains three of PReP's dispatches, which focus on causes, responses, and preventive efforts linked to revolutionary transformation. Another important manifesto/pamphlet in the Moving Beyond Capitalism – Now! series also addresses important complementary themes: *Abolitionist Agroecology, Food Sovereignty and Pandemic Prevention*, by Maywa Montenegro de Wit.

The first dispatch presented here is "Globalized food systems, structural inequality, and COVID-19," written by Rob Wallace and submitted from the PReP Outbreak Origins subgroup. As an evolutionary epidemiologist, Rob has studied for over two decades how agricultural corporations "farm pathogens" leading to epidemics through destruction of natural habitat and through industrial production of meat. In the creation of capitalist, globalized food systems, patterns of structural inequality based on social class hierarchies and racism become ever more apparent and problematic. This dispatch gives an helpful overview of these conditions, from the perspective of early during the COVID-19 pandemic.

In "What is mutual aid? A COVID-19 primer," members of the PReP Neighborhoods subgroup analyze the transformative process of mutual aid. Communities around the world have carried out pathbreaking mutual aid projects in response to the overwhelming needs for food, housing, and services that arose during the pandemic due to a lack of adequate safety nets in capitalist countries. They trace the origins of mutual aid in anarchist thought and practice, including that of the biologist and "revolutionist" Peter Kropotkin. In his influential study of cooperation among animals, Kropotkin showed that mutual aid, rather than only competition among species, emerged as an important benefit in biological evolution. Carefully distinguishing between mutual aid and charity, the PReP dispatch emphasizes that mutual aid aims toward societal transformation beyond the injustices of racial capitalism. They describe the important components of revolutionary mutual aid practices that have emerged during the pandemic throughout the world, with detailed examples from groups like Southern Solidarity in New Orleans.

"Can agroecology stop COVID-21, -22, and -23? Moving Beyond Capitalist Agriculture," produced by members of the PReP Agroecologies subgroup, provides concrete steps to achieve a post-capitalist, non-exploitative, anti-racist, sustainable, and joyful process of food production. This approach also has the tremendous advantage of restoring natural habitat and reducing industrial production of meat, which are key goals in changing the dangerous conditions of capitalist agriculture that cause pandemics. An important theme is that peasant- and indigenous-led agroecology limits the spread of zoonotic viruses by protecting agricultural biodiversity and enhancing food sovereignty.

The inspiring, multifaceted work of PReP scientists and activists points our way to a revolutionary transformation of agriculture and public health. Their path-breaking observations about the relationships among capitalist industrial agriculture, habitat destruction, and emerging epidemics and pandemics have focused attention on the upstream causes of pandemics, rooted in the structures of racial capitalism that have shaped the global production and distribution of food. Such structural conditions cannot be modified by technological solutions such as vaccines or medications or by piecemeal reforms. Through their scientific work and their political praxis, those who participate in PReP are providing crucial leadership and hope in transforming some of the most important components of the enormous crisis that confronts our planet and its inhabitants. We are grateful for the opportunity of facilitating these crucial efforts through this publication, and we invite your participation.

Globalized Food Systems, Structural Inequality, and COVID-19

Rob Wallace
PReP Outbreak Origins

The following is the revised text of a talk PReP's Rob Wallace originally gave on April 16, 2020, at a Transnational Institute webinar in conversation with organizers Moayyad Bsharat, Arie Kurniawaty, Sai Sam, and Paula Gioia from, respectively, Palestine, Indonesia, Myanmar, and Germany by way of Brazil. The presenters talked through how SARS-CoV-2, the COVID virus, evolved out of the very structural inequalities it is also now exacerbating. The webinar is available in full here: https://www.youtube.com/watch?v=m9A6WkeqPss.

Thank you very much. It's a pleasure to be here in spite of our present circumstances.

Inequalities in outcomes based on different policies and practices

Let's begin with the status of the pandemic. The Johns Hopkins global map has us this morning at 5.5 million confirmed COVID cases worldwide and 350,000 dead.[1] Given the counts some countries are reporting as suspected cases, this confirmed caseload is likely 5 to 10 times an underestimate.[2] So at worst as many as 50 million people have to this point been infected – some more critically than others. For the worse outcomes – with uneven testing across the globe and some areas stretched to medical capacity – deaths are also likely undercounted.[3]

More than a quarter of the confirmed cases have been situated in the United States, with large outbreaks in Europe and the Middle East. The global South already began its own run up the epicurve, in a context of comparatively lesser public health capacity, fewer household resources for sheltering-in-place, and a wider array of underlying co-morbidities – that is, other health conditions that can complicate a COVID infection.[4] Indeed, as occurred for the HIV epidemic, in the most impoverished areas of both global North and South, other matters – including getting enough food to eat – may be more pressing than what many infected may gamble is only a passing shortness of breath.[5]

That all said, COVID isn't merely business as usual. We see some telling reversals. Britain accepted shipments of masks from Vietnam.[6] Cuba sent doctors to NATO member Italy.[7] And Senegal turned around COVID tests in four hours, while in the U.S. such tests, even when available, were taking up to ten days.[8]

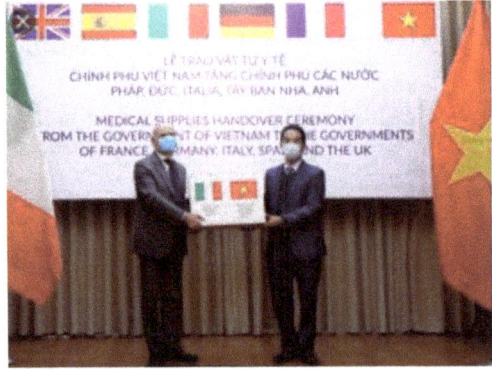

Vietnam's Deputy Foreign Minister To Anh Dung hands a box of masks to Italy's Ambassador to Vietnam Antonio Alessandro.

These telltales are underway during what the world-systems theorists describe as a major shift in the prevalent cycles of capital accumulation that have structured much of the world order the past 500 years.[9] The pandemic serves as much as a marker of such a shift as a shockingly immediate crisis. The United States, on the tail end of its cycle of accumulation, turning capital back to money for the wealthiest – that is, cashing out – is, outside its military budget, no longer newly investing in the infrastructure of global empire.

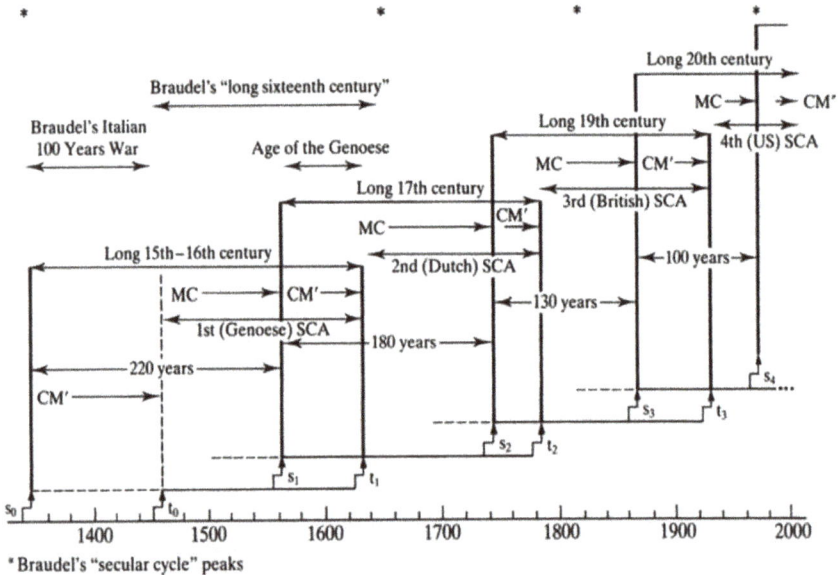

* Braudel's "secular cycle" peaks

World-systems theorist Giovanni Arrighi's riff on Fernand Braudel. Capital accumulation – MC, money to capital – followed by busts of serial empire cashing out – CM', capital to money: the Italian city states, Spain not shown here, the Dutch, the British empire, and the U.S. century.

U.S. power, for instance, was until this outbreak on the hook for cleaning up pandemics that capital the world over helped create.[10] The U.S. tasked itself with keeping the global system on the same developmental path despite the ultimately unsustainable (and hideous) destruction to land and people that path represents. So defunding the World Health Organization, as the U.S. did, wasn't an exercise in imperial might.[11] It was a white flag, a capitulation.

Domestically, the U.S. failures to respond to its own outbreak were more than missteps by the Trump administration, and were programmed in decades ago as the shared commons of public health were simultaneously neglected and sold off.[12] A country captured by a regimen of individualized, just-in-time epidemiology – an utter contradiction – with barely enough hospital beds and equipment for normal operations, was unable to marshal the resources necessary to pursue the scale of disease suppression that a COVID outbreak demands.

Indeed, many a New Yorker denied access to a critical care bed and then gasping for breath on their couches at home had much more in common with a West African infected with Ebola in a structurally adjusted health care system than with any other New Yorker wealthy enough to pay for medical care on demand.[13] Nearly two thousand New Yorkers were found dead in their homes the first eight days of April 2020.[14]

Rural areas also got pummeled.[15] Louisa County in Iowa, home to a Tyson company meat packing plant through which COVID burned right through, at one point hosted more cases per capita than New York State.[16] The county, home to 11,000 people, had neither a hospital nor a practicing physician living there.

China, in contrast, is on the front end of its cycle of accumulation.[17] It is invested in building the infrastructure, including global public health, it needs to turn money into capital (and imperial might). Such a transition – U.S. to China – is neither assured nor absolves China of its public health ills, including producing conditions for COVID-19's very emergence as we'll discuss further.[18] But we should note that the structural impulse there is different. Indeed, upon an initial stumble, China moved to eradicate COVID from Hubei, the province of origin, by deploying 40,000 medical staff from other provinces and conducting comprehensive contact tracing and testing.[19] China donated millions in U.S. dollars to its African trade partners to fight COVID.[20]

Beyond this contrast of two giants, the question of why some countries escaped the worst of the outbreak is worth comment. There was a matter

Retweet of Vietnam Ministry of Health contact tracing for international flights with documented COVID-19 case onboard. Hotline number provided. Contrast the response with the Trump announcement that scared home phalanxes of Americans in Europe, crowded through airports without testing or follow-up.

of geography. How close to an epicenter? South America and Africa started up late this way. But even countries bordering China escaped the worst of it. It helps if a government both prepares the country during the advance warning it's been given and sees the shared commons as still part of the purview of governance.

Taiwan, for instance, tested people at the airport for COVID-19, disinfected their suitcases, drove each person separately to their destination in a government-provided taxi, and gave each arrival one phone app that tells them where in their area they're staying that they could purchase a mask and another app that listed local infections and their case histories.[21]

Iceland aggressively tested its population and isolated the positive cases.[22] It deployed detectives to contact-trace any infection. Those in contact with a case were also sequestered, so that if any of these people proved to be infected, they were already in quarantine. The rest of the country went about its business, walking free outside without masks.

Vietnam provided comprehensive health care to nearly the entirety of its population, and, unlike, say, Louisa County in Iowa, had doctors and nurses in every community.[23] Along with the typical border protocols, like China, whole buildings were quarantined should a case be detected but the building's occupants were provided three meals a day for a small charge. Apartment buildings hosted whole-body sanitizing stations at all entrances.[24] Empty hotels were used as quarantine sites, where doctors made house calls. Everybody wore a mask. And unlike the U.S., where the federal government set off a black market bidding war for ventilators among its states, there were few if any reports from Vietnam of price gouging, panic buying, or hoarding.[25]

That said, *all* countries were in for a rough ride with the global economy already falling toward a recession before the outbreak began.[26] Those countries pummeled worst by the pandemic found themselves farther in the fiscal hole. In an effort to fix outbreak and economy at the same time, the grim calculus of capital attempted to push the two crises of its own making onto the indigenous and the poorest workers worldwide. Brazil under Bolsonaro even before the Amazonian fires showed that calculus.[27] But also, in the U.S., the government aimed to reduce the already criminal wages that immigrant farmworkers were making as "pandemic relief" for agricultural companies.[28]

Industrial agriculture and pandemics

Our cycles of accumulation – the U.S. cashing out and China ramping up – impacted COVID's very origins. Over the past forty years, China chose to engage in massive shifts in land use and migration to domestically feed and pay its population.[29] These shifts had considerable impact in decoupling (and recoupling) traditional ecologies into new configurations that had a profound effect on economy and epidemiology alike. So we see post-economic liberalization, the rise of multiple strains of new influenzas, including H5N1, H6N1, H7N9, and H9N2, as well as SARS-1 and, now, an explosion in cases of African Swine fever which killed half of China's hogs in 2019.[30]

There is some controversy as to COVID's local origins, but the genetics of the virus – SARS-CoV-2 – show it to be recombinant of a bat coronavirus and a pangolin strain that subsequently went through some

Hogs culled for African Swine Fever dumped in Hong Kong, May 2019.

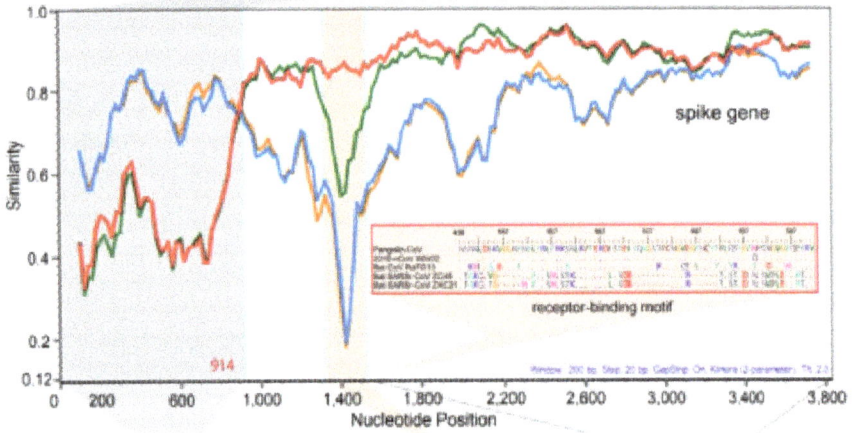

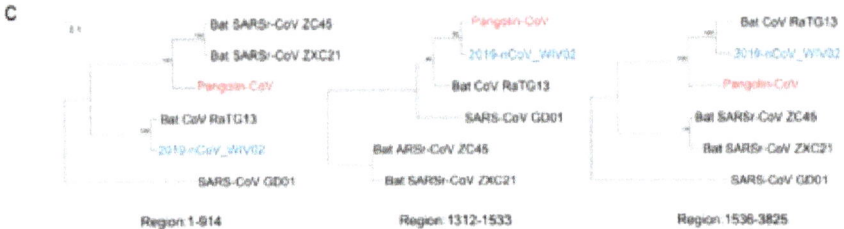

Similarity plot of the genetics of a pangolin strain of SARS with SARS-CoV-2 ("2019-nCoV") and a series of bat coronaviruses. Most of the SARS-2 genome is similar to bat SARS sample CoV RaTG13, although another bat strain from Yunnan has since been shown to be related more closely. But it's in the spike gene of the receptor-binding domain that SARS-2 uses to get into the human cell where SARS-2 is more similar to the pangolin strain. That indicates some recombination event occurred, when the pangolin strain spike gene transferred into the bat background before the strain adapted to the human receptor and went human-to-human. From Xiao et al. reference in end note 31.

attuning to the human immune system whether before or upon the Wuhan outbreak.[31] But clearly agriculture had a role to play in this process even if that central Wuhan market didn't. Somehow the virus got from one of the many coronaviruses documented to circulate among a variety of bat species in Central China into Wuhan proper.[32] To claim agriculture had no impact, as China is moving toward as an official position, or absurdly, that the virus didn't originate in China at all, would position opponents of agriculture's role in a pretty precarious position.[33] How to explain the move from bats through pangolins through perhaps another intermediate species such as hogs into humans without bringing up agriculture (or logging or mining)? The genetics don't support a lab accident.[34]

In all likelihood an expanding regional circuit of production maneuvered both the increasingly formalized wild foods sector and industrial livestock production further into the hinterlands where both sectors increasingly encountered bat reservoirs.[35] Periurban loops of growing

Seizures of illegal shipments of pangolin scales, 2000-2019, from some of the supply staging areas in Indochina and market targets in southern China (although that doesn't preclude use outside of China as well). There is in addition an increasing push to farm the notoriously difficult to cultivate but lucrative pangolin. https://eia-international.org/wildlife/wildlife-trade-maps/illegal-trade-seizures-pangolins/.

extent and population density can increase the interface (and spillover) between wild nonhuman populations and newly urbanized rural areas. Those new geographies also reduce the kind of environmental complexity with which forests can disrupt the transmission of deadly viruses as we would like our forests to do.[36]

That regional circuit of production of COVID's likely origins – forest through periurban to city – is reproduced around the world.[37] This scenario offers a broader framework by which to organize our thinking about outbreaks nearly everywhere – not just China. SARS 1 and 2, Ebola, Zika, yellow fever, African swine fever, avian and swine influenzas, Nipah virus, Q fever, among others, and, historically, HIV, all originated or re-emerged somewhere along such expanding circuits of production, whether in the forest, in the new periurban continuum, or in factory farms or processing plants near or in cities. Many such new ecologies are driven by imperial or neoliberal imposition.[38] Clearly infectious diseases aren't merely matters of the virus itself, but also the context in which they emerge.[39]

Indeed, looking toward the future, we find coronavises are only one of many pathogens developing in such an agroeconomic context. What we are suffering today is already also in motion somewhere else, many times over, like viral hurricanes lining up in the Atlantic Ocean.

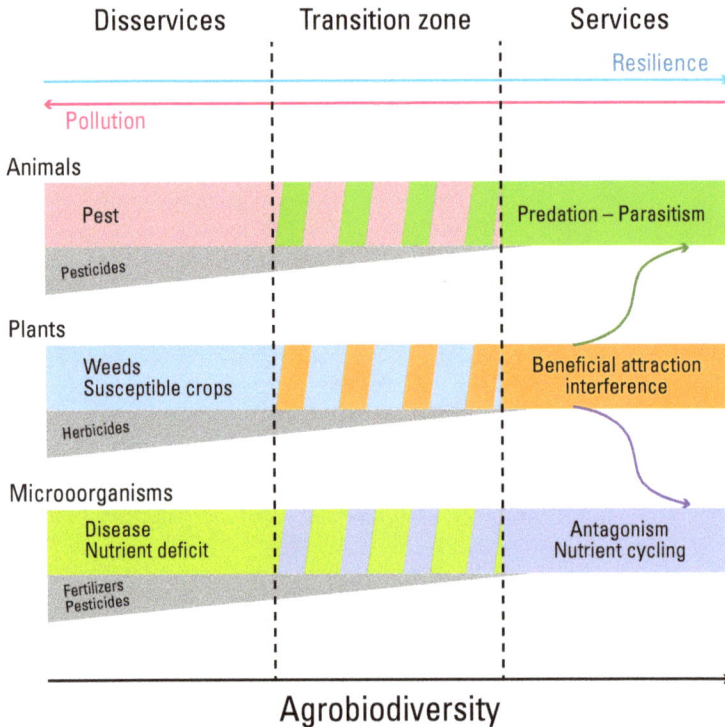

Agrobiodiversity promotes ecological services. The diversities promote healthier soils, beneficial insects, and pest predators, decreasing the need for agricultural inputs such as pesticides and fertilizers that pollute local environments and capture the near-entirety of farmer income. Diversities reintroduce genetic mosaics that help block the spread of pathogens at both the farm and region levels. From Corrado et al. in end note 47.

Agroecology, habitat restoration, pandemic prevention

What to do? As perhaps a prompt for our conversation today, I'll touch upon some possibilities if only as a series of questions.

Are we prepared to rebuild the town economies that permit farmers and fisher folk around the world the autonomy they need to source local inputs without destroying wilderness?[40] Can we learn to learn from indigenous groups how to treat a landscape as much as a matter of our ethos as a source of food?[41]

Will we finally abandon settler ideologies? Will we reintroduce ourselves back into Earth's cycles of regeneration?[42] Can we rediscover our sense of individuation – who we are – in multitudes of people beyond what capital and the state offer us?[43]

Are we prepared to fight to reclaim rural and forest landscapes and local waters that agribusiness has turned into sacrifice zones for global capital?[44] Will we aim to defeat agribusiness as both a mode of production and a political opponent – from its lobbying in State capitols to its campaigns in killing environmental activists along neoliberal frontiers of the forest edge?[45]

I believe these questions are the fires we must walk through in order to be able to introduce the now suddenly-obvious strategies in pandemic prevention:

Among them, we need to protect the forest complexity that keeps deadly pathogens from lining up livestock and human hosts for a straight shot onto the world's travel network.[46] We need to reintroduce the livestock and crop diversities, and reintegrate animal and crop farming at scales that keep pathogens from ramping up in deadliness.[47] We must once again allow our food animals to reproduce onsite, restarting the natural selection that allows immune evolution to track pathogens in real time.

In short, what to do includes many of the very practices the indigenous and smallholders of the world engage in as a matter of course in their everyday cultivation.[48] Can we scale these out specific to the needs of people and place? Can we, as the Zapatistas have been paraphrased, can we make *un mundo donde quepan muchos mundos*?[49] – a world where many worlds fit?

27 May 2020

Robert G. Wallace is an evolutionary epidemiologist at the Agroecology and Rural Economics Research Corps. He is author of *Dead Epidemiologists: On the Origins of COVID-19*, and *Big Farms Make Big Flu*; and co-author of *Neoliberal Ebola: Modeling Disease Emergence from Finance to Forest and Farm*, and *Clear-Cutting Disease Control: Capital-Led Deforestation, Public Health Austerity, and Vector-Borne Infection*. He has consulted for the Food and Agriculture Organization and the Centers for Disease Control.

Pandemic Research for the People is a crowd-funded effort aimed at conducting research on questions that will directly help communities around the world during the ongoing COVID-19 pandemic. For more information or to donate to the project, please visit the PReP website: https://arerc.wordpress.com/pandemic-research-for-the- people/.

Contact. Feel free to contact PReP at https://arerc.wordpress.com/contact/ or preporganizer@gmail.com.

These dispatches are intended as provocative and informative commentary aimed at galvanizing new thinking around the present pandemic and its causes. The views in this dispatch represent those of the author and not necessarily those of Pandemic Research for the People.

References

1. Coronavirus Resource Center (2020) World Map, 25 May. COVID-19 Dashboard by the Center for Systems Science and Engineering (CSSE) at Johns Hopkins University. https://coronavirus.jhu.edu/map.html.
2. Li D, J Lv, G Botwin, J Braun, W Cao, L Li, and DPB McGovern (2020) Estimating the scale of COVID-19 epidemic in the United States: Simulations based on air traffic directly from Wuhan, China. MedRxiv, 8 March. https://www.medrxiv.org/content/10.1101/2020.03.06.20031880v1. article-info; Zhongwei Jia and Zuhong Lu (2020) Modelling COVID-19 transmission: from data to intervention. *Lancet Infect Dis*. doi: 10.1016/S1473- 3099(20)30258-9
3. Wu J, A McCann, J Katz, and E Peltier (2020) 74,000 missing deaths: Tracking the true toll of the coronavirus outbreak. *New York Times*, 19 May. https://www.nytimes.com/interactive/2020/04/21/world/coronavirus- missing-deaths.html.
4. Ndii D (2020) Thoughts on a pandemic, geoeconomics and Africa's urban sociology. *The Elephant*, 25 March. https://www.theelephant.info/op-eds/2020/03/25/thoughts-on-a-pandemic-geoeconomics-and-africas-urban- sociology/; Kapara N, C Ihekweazu, F Ntoumi, et al. (2020) Is Africa prepared for tackling the COVID-19 (SARS- CoV-2) epidemic. Lessons from past outbreaks, ongoing pan-African public health efforts, and implications for the future. International Journal of Infectious Diseases, 93:233-236; Gilbert M, G Pullano, F Pinotti, E Valdano, et al. Preparedness and vulnerability of African countries against importations of COVID-19: a modelling study. *The Lancet*, 395(102777):871-877.
5. Zurayk R (2020) Pandemic and food security: A view from the Global South. *Journal of Agriculture, Food Systems, and Community Development*, 9(3). https://foodsystemsjournal.org/index.php/fsj/article/view/803/789.
6. Cockburn H (2020) Vietnamese children donate 20,000 face masks to UK after saving up 'lucky money'. The Independent, 24 April. https://www.independent.co.uk/news/uk/home-news/vietnamese-children-donate-face- masks-uk-coronavirus-ppe-shortage-a9483276.html.
7. Augustin E (2020) Cuba has sent 2,000 doctors and nurses overseas to fight Covid-19. *The Nation*, 22 May. https://www.thenation.com/article/world/cuba-doctors-covid-19/.
8. Lange J (2020) Senegal is reportedly turning coronavirus tests around 'within 4 hours' while Americans might wait a week. Yahoo News, 12 March. https://news.yahoo.com/senegal-reportedly-turning-coronavirus-tests- 165224221.html; Shryock R (2020) Senegal pledges a bed for every coronavirus patient – and their contacts, too. NPR, 17 May. https://www.npr.org/sections/goatsandsoda/2020/05/17/856016429/senegal-pledges-a-bed-for- every-coronavirus-patient-and-their-contacts-too.
9. Arrighi G (1994 [2010]). *The Long Twentieth Century: Money, Power and the Origins of Our Times*. Verso, London.
10. Tharoor I (2020) Trump's pandemic response underscores the crisis in global politics. *Washington Post*, 16 April. https://www.washingtonpost.com/world/2020/04/17/trumps-pandemic-response-underscores-crisis-global- politics/
11. Allen L (2020) Defunding the WHO was a calculated decision, not an impromptu tweet. *The Conversation*, 20 April. https://theconversation.com/defunding-the-who-was-a-calculated-decision-not-an-impromptu-tweet- 136620.
12. Waitzkin H (ed) (2018) *Health Care Under the Knife: Moving Beyond Capitalism for Our Health*. Monthly Review Press, New York.
13. Wallace RG and R Wallace (eds) (2016) *Neoliberal Ebola: Modeling Disease Emergence from Finance to Forest and Farm*. Springer, Cham.
14. Watkins A and WK Rashbaum (2020) How many people have actually died from coronavirus in New York? New York Times, 10 April. https://www.nytimes.com/2020/04/10/nyregion/new-york-coronavirus-death-count.html.
15. Thebault R and A Hauslohner (2020) Covid-19's deadly new surge is in rural America as states re-open. *Washington Post*, 24 May. https://www.washingtonpost.com/nation/2020/05/24/coronavirus-rural-america- outbreaks/?arc404=true.
16. Rynard P (2020) Louisa County COVID-19 rate now worse than New York State. *Iowa Starting Line*, 13 April. https://iowastartingline.com/2020/04/13/louisa-county-covid-19-rate-now-worse-than-new-york-state/.
17. Arrighi G (2007) *Adam Smith in Beijing: Lineages Of The 21st Century*. Verso, New York.
18. Gulick J (2011) The Long Twentieth Century and barriers to China's hegemonic accession. *Journal of World-Systems Research*, 17(1):4-38.
19. Brueck H, AM Miller, and S Feder (2020) China took at least 12 strict measures to control the coronavirus. They could work for the US, but would likely be impossible to implement. *Business Insider*, 24 March. https://www.businessinsider.com/chinas-coronavirus-quarantines-other-countries-arent-ready-2020-3.
20. Marques CF (2020) China in Africa is more than a land grab: Beijing is after political influence, and its coronavirus aid will count for much. *Bloomberg*, 27 April. https://www.bloomberg.com/opinion/articles/2020-04-27/china-s- coronavirus-aid-to-africa-will-build-political-support.
21. Wang CJ, CY Ng, and RH Brook (2020) Response to COVID-19 in Taiwan: Big data analytics, new technology, and proactive testing. *JAMA*, 323(14):1321-1342.

22. Marx W and MW Bishop (2020) Iceland employs detective work, testing and quarantine in coronavirus fight. NBC News, 27 March. https://www.nbcnews.com/news/world/iceland-employs-detective-work-testing-and-quarantine- coronavirus-fight-n1170166.
23. Le SM (2020) Containing the coronavirus (COVID-19): Lessons from Vietnam. *World Bank Blogs*, 30 April. https://blogs.worldbank.org/health/containing-coronavirus-covid-19-lessons-vietnam.
24. Thanh N (2020) Covid-19 innovation: Vietnam's mobile chambers allow disinfection in one go. *VN Express*, 16 March. https://e.vnexpress.net/news/news/covid-19-innovation-vietnam-s-mobile-chambers-allow-disinfection- in-one-go-4069276.html.
25. Ashwill MA (2020) Vietnam: An outlier in the coronavirus epidemic and HE? *University World News*, 14 March. https://www.universityworldnews.com/post.php?story=20200313063615630.
26. Roberts M (2020) It was the virus that did it. *Michael Roberts Blog*, 15 March. https://thenextrecession.wordpress.com/2020/03/15/it-was-the-virus-that-did-it/.
27. Diele-Viegas LM and CFD Rocha (2020) Why releasing mining on Amazonian indigenous lands and the advance of agrobusiness is extremely harmful for the mitigation of world's climate change? Comment on Pereira et al. (*Environmental Science & Policy* 100 (2019) 8–12). Environmental Science & Policy, 103:30-31; Londoño E and L Casado (2020) As Bolsonaro keeps Amazon vows, Brazil's Indigenous fear 'ethnocide'. *New York Times*, 19 April. https://www.nytimes.com/2020/04/19/world/americas/bolsonaro-brazil-amazon-indigenous.html.
28. Ordoñez F (2020) White House seeks to lower farmworker pay to help agriculture industry. NPR News, 10 April. https://www.npr.org/2020/04/10/832076074/white-house-seeks-to-lower-farmworker-pay-to-help-agriculture- industry.
29. Wallace RG, L Bergmann, L Hogerwerf, and M Gilbert (2010) Are influenzas in southern China byproducts of the region's globalising historical present? In S Craddock, T Giles-Vernick, and J Gunn (eds) *Influenza and Public Health: Learning from Past Pandemics*. EarthScan Press, London.
30. Liu Q, L Cao, and X-Q Zhu (2014) Major emerging and re-emerging zoonoses in China: a matter of global health and socioeconomic development for 1.3 billion. *International Journal of Infectious Diseases*, 25:65-72; Vergne T, C Chen-Fu, S Li, J Cappelle, J Edwards, et al. (2017) Pig empire under infectious threat: risk of African swine fever introduction into the People's Republic of China. *Vet Record*, 181(5):117.
31. Andersen KG, A Rambaut, WI Lipkin, and EC Holmes. The proximal origin of SARS-CoV-2. *Nature Medicine*, 26:450-452; Xiao K, J Zhai, Y Feng, N Zhou, X Zhang, et al. (2020) Isolation and characterization of 2019-nCoV- like coronavirus from Malayan pangolins. bioRxiv. https://www.biorxiv.org/content/10.1101/2020.02.17.951335v1.
32. Wu Z, L Yang, X Ren, G He, J Zhang, et al. (2016) Deciphering the bat virome catalog to better understand the ecological diversity of bat viruses and the bat origin of emerging infectious diseases. *ISME J*, 10(3):609-620.
33. Choy G, T Ng, B Jaipragas, J Ma, and Z Pinghi (2020) South Korea tops China for first time. South China Morning Post, 27 Feburary. https://www.scmp.com/news/china/society/article/3052577/coronavirus-south-korea- infections-could-exceed-china-which.
34. Andersen KG, A Rambaut, WI Lipkin, and EC Holmes. The proximal origin of SARS-CoV-2.
35. Field HE (2009) Bats and emerging zoonoses: Henipaviruses and SARS. *Zoonoses and Public Health*, 56(6-7):278- 284; Afelt A, R Frutos, and C Devaux (2018) Bats, Coronaviruses, and deforestation: Toward the emergence of novel infectious diseases? *Frontiers in Microbiology*, 9:702; Wallace RG, A Liebman, LF Chaves, and R Wallace (2020) COVID-19 and circuits of capital. *Monthly Review*, 72(1). https://monthlyreview.org/2020/05/01/covid- 19-and-circuits-of-capital/; Wallace RG (2020) Midvinter-19. Patreon, 5 May. https://www.patreon.com/posts/midvinter-19-36797182; Fisher G (2020) Deforestation and monoculture farming spread COVID-19 and other diseases. *TruthOut*, 12 May. https://truthout.org/articles/deforestation-and-monoculture-farming-spread-covid-19-and-other-diseases/.
36. Wallace R, LF Chaves, LR Bergmann, C Ayres, L Hogerwerf, R Kock, and RG Wallace (2018) *Clear-Cutting Disease Control: Capital-Led Deforestation, Public Health Austerity, and Vector-Borne Infection*. Springer, Switzerland.
37. Wallace RG, A Liebman, LF Chaves, and R Wallace (2020) COVID-19 and circuits of capital; Wallace RG (2021) Agriculture, capital, and infectious diseases. In Hans Harren, et al., *IAASTD – Ten Years After*. In press.
38. Wallace RG and R Wallace (eds) (2016) *Neoliberal Ebola: Modeling Disease Emergence from Finance to Forest and Farm*.
39. Wallace RG (2016) *Big Farms Make Big Flu*. Monthly Review Press, New York.
40. IPES-Food (2016) *From Uniformity to Diversity: A Paradigm Shift from Industrial Agriculture to Diversified Agroecological Systems*. Louvain-la-Neuve, Belgium. http://www.ipes- food.org/_img/upload/files/UniformityToDiversity_FULL.pdf; IPES-Food (2018) Breaking Away from Industrial Food and Farming Systems: Seven Case Studies of Agroecological Transition. Louvain-la-Neuve, Belgium. http://www.ipes-food.org/_img/upload/files/CS2_web.pdf; Chappell, M.J (2018) *Beginning to End Hunger: Food and the Environment in Belo Horizonte, Brazil, and Beyond*. University of California Press, Berkeley; Arias PF, T Jonas, and K Munksgaard (eds) (2019) *Farming Democracy: Radically Transforming the Food System from the Ground Up;* Australian Food Sovereignty Alliance. Vivero-Pol JL, T Ferrando, O De Schutter, and U Mattei (eds) (2019) *Routledge Handbook of Food as a Commons*. Routledge, New York; Giraldo OF (2019) *Political Ecology of Agriculture: Agroecology and Post-Development*. Springer, Cham.

41. Suárez-Torres J, J Ricardo Suárez-López, D López-Paredes, H Morocho, LE Cachiguango-Cachiguango, and W Dellai (2017) Agroecology and health: Lessons from Indigenous populations. *Current Environmental Health Reports,* 4:244–25; Pascoe B (2018) *Dark Emu: Aboriginal Australia and the Birth of Agriculture.* Scribe, London; Figueroa-Helland L, C Thomas, and AP Aguilera (2018) Decolonizing food systems: Food sovereignty, indigenous revitalization, and agroecology as counter-hegemonic movements. *Perspectives on Global Development and Technology,* 17(1-2):173-201.

42. Mandel E (1970) Progressive disalienation through the building of socialist society, or the inevitable alienation in industrial dociety? In *The Marxist Theory of Alienation.* Pathfinder, New York; Foster JB (2018) Marx, value, and nature. Monthly Review, 70(3):122-136; Wallace RG, K Okamoto, and A Liebman (2021) Earth, the alien planet. In DB Monk and M Sorkin (eds) *Between Catastrophe and Redemption: Essays in Honor of Mike Davis.* OR Books, New York. In press.

43. Virno P (2004) *A Grammar of the Multitude.* Semiotext(e), Los Angeles; Federici S (2018) *Re-enchanting the World: Feminism and the Politics of the Commons.* PM, Oakland.

44. Oliveira G and S Hecht (2016) Sacred groves, sacrifice zones and soy production: globalization, intensification and neo-nature in South America. *Journal of Peasant Studies,* 43:251-285; Edelman M (2019) Hollowed out Heartland, USA: How capital sacrificed communities and paved the way for authoritarian populism. *Journal of Rural Studies.* https://www.sciencedirect.com/science/article/abs/pii/S0743016719305157.

45. Wallace R, L Hogerwerf, A Liebman, L Bergmann, and RG Wallace. Agribusiness vs. public health: Disease control in resource-asymmetric conflict. Preprint available at https://hal.archives-ouvertes.fr/hal-02513883.

46. Wallace R, LF Chaves, LR Bergmann, C Ayres, L Hogerwerf, R Kock, and RG Wallace (2018) *Clear-Cutting Disease Control: Capital-Led Deforestation, Public Health Austerity, and Vector-Borne Infection.*

47. Corrado C, T Elena, R Giancarlo, and C Stefano (2019) The role of agrobiodiversity in sustainable food systems design and management. In D Nandwani (ed), *Genetic Diversity in Horticultural Plants.* Springer, Cham, pp 245-271; Wallace RG, A Liebman, D Weisberger, T Jonas, L Bergmann, R Kock, and R Wallace (In press) Industrial agricultural environments. In J Fall, R Francis, MA Schlaepfer, and K Barker (eds) *The Routledge Handbook of Biosecurity and Invasive Species.* Routledge, New York.

48. Kremen C, A Iles, and C Bacon (2012) Diversified farming systems: An agroecological, systems-based alternative to modern industrial agriculture. Ecology and Society, 17(4):44; Magne M-A, G Martin, M Moraine, J Ryschawy, V Thenard et al. (2019) An integrated approach to livestock farming systems' autonomy to design and manage agroecological transition at the farm and territorial levels. In J-E Bergez, E Audouin, and O Therond (eds) *Agroecological Transitions: From Theory to Practice in Local Participatory Design.* Springer, Cham, pp 45-68.

49. EZLN-CCRI (2005) *Sixth Declaration of the Lacandon Jungle (Sexta DecDeLaSelva-Espanol-Booklet. pdf; Ortega FIM and FA Zañartu Toloza (2017) Un mundo donde quepan muchos mundos: Neozapatismo y el EZLN en México.* Revista Espacios & Memorias, Nº 2. Universidad Metropolitana de Ciencias de la Educación, Chile.

What is mutual aid?

A COVID-19 PRIMER

John Gulick, Jasmine Araujo, Cora Roelofs, Tanya Kerssen,
Meleiza Figueroa, Etant Dupain, Serena Stein, Deborah Wallace,
Ryan Petteway, John Choe, Luca de Crescenzo, Audrey Snyder,
Colin Kloecker, and Rob Wallace

PReP Neighborhoods

PReP Neighborhoods, our working group dedicated to the research needs of neighborhoods the world over during the present pandemic, met for the first time in late April 2020. Before jumping into specific practices and protocols that neighborhood groups might consider implementing, the group decided it would be best to start out by exploring what mutual aid means in our present context. It may not be what you think.

The COVID-19 pandemic has strained and even overwhelmed the public health, medical care, and disaster response systems where governments and state agencies were ill-prepared to contain and suppress infectious outbreaks.[1] In countries where emergency lockdown measures have been adopted without accompanying policies to guarantee income security and housing tenure, there is the additional problem of economic hardship.[2] Already existing and newly formed non-governmental organizations and associations have mobilized to fill the gap.[3]

These formal and informal groups assist people forced into the margins by government neglect with free meals, grocery and medicine deliveries, safe housing, and even cash. The groups go beyond traditional voluntary charity disaster relief to provide personal protective equipment (notably face masks), COVID-19 symptoms monitoring, accurate information about locally available COVID-19 and antibody testing facilities, emotional counseling, and more.[4] In some cases, these organizations partner with public agencies, including in situations where state institutions are both omnipresent and capable and voluntary associations are essentially licensed subcontractors of the state (as appears to be the case, but only in part, in the People's Republic of China).[5]

In other contexts – particularly where robust social safety nets are lacking or where austerity has undermined any expectation of government assistance – people have done what they have always done in a crisis: attempted to stem the tide of misery with the resources they have.[6]

Members of Southern Solidarity, a mutual aid group in New Orleans.

Some of these organizations or associations of individuals are describing their efforts to help those in trouble as "mutual aid organizations."[7] These groups reflect the social or political philosophies of their founders and members, from a devotion to principles of community self-help (in both its conservative and radical variants) to a belief that systematically oppressed groups best overcome their oppression through collective self-management and self-provisioning. They distinguish themselves from charity organizations by their lack of formal association with either the government or the non-profit or religious charity sector and identify as just people helping other people in need.[8]

In New Orleans, for example, a mutual aid group mobilized by Jasmine Araujo and called Southern Solidarity has emerged, guided by Black feminist liberation thought and inspired by the direct relief and organizing practices of the Black Panther Party.[9] The group of about 30 organize the daily delivery of food, medical resources, and other basic needs directly to about 300 unhoused people in the downtown area of New Orleans

Jasmine Aruajo

because the government failed to meet these needs.[10] Southern Solidarity is involved in both direct relief and consciousness raising efforts of members and recipients. Members act on the principle that when those who are oppressed get their needs met, they are better equipped to move from survival mode to organizing. Key members include trans activists, organizers, formerly incarcerated people, and the unhoused.

What is mutual aid?

Mutual aid as a political concept is drawn from the work of anarchist and scientist Peter Kropotkin. In 1902, Kropotkin published *Mutual Aid: A Factor in Evolution*, which argued that it was human cooperation and not competition which has facilitated the survival of our species.[11] Additionally, Kropotkin proposed that the best system of economic and social organization would be one based on mutual exchanges rather than coercion and the profit-motive.

Mutual aid societies or "benevolent societies" have long arisen among disenfranchised groups to fill gaps in insurance, support, education, and relief. Examples include the Free African Society formed in late 18th century Philadelphia by formerly enslaved men and contemporary organizations of refugees and immigrants such as the Cambodian Mutual Assistance Association in Lowell, Massachusetts, where members gather and share resources to face shared challenges.[12]

The labor movement was founded on the principle of collective organization for mutual benefit of its members and helped politicize such assistance as acts of solidarity not charity. The radical edges of the labor movement, as represented by the Industrial Workers of the World, broke through the "in-group" orientation of mutual aid efforts with their slogan "An injury to one is an injury to all."[13] While the Black Panther Party's Free Breakfast Program was an acknowledged charity operation in response to the poverty imposed upon Black people in the United States, the Panthers viewed it as facilitating the development of a revolutionary people.[14] In short, people who are in need of basic necessities such as food cannot effectively rebel until they have those needs met.

In light of budget austerity and the shredding of social services, mutual aid has become a term loosely applied to all kinds of charity supplied by voluntary organizations.[15] For those of us interested in *liberatory* mutual aid, it's crucial to carefully consider what should be the standards for such efforts. An emancipatory mutual aid is not only about connecting those in need to services or even directly providing services, but also about organizing with those in need to assert their human rights and demand what is socially just from systems of exploitation and domination.

In the spirit of the Zapatista principle of *mandar obedeciendo* ("to lead, obeying"), efforts must be made to assure that the agency and voice of those receiving aid are equal to, or even ahead of, those providing it, despite the apparent disparity in resources.[16] An impressive example of a large-scale mutual aid endeavor during the COVID-19 crisis comes from a favela of 100,000 people in São Paulo, Brazil.[17] There, 400 "presidents" each took responsibility for the welfare of 50 families apiece, tracking COVID-19 symptoms in family members, and preparing and distributing thousands of hot meals every day.[18]

Radical mutual aid aims to open up space for those forced into dispossession to interrogate why it is that those providing resources are in possession of such resources and those receiving them are not, and also to question why those providing resources are providing them.

That is, one component of mutual aid at its best is education and consciousness-raising about power relations – not only the relations between mutual aid donors, distributors, and beneficiaries, but also the power dynamics that structure political and economic conditions and social

Members of Southern Solidarity, a mutual aid group in New Orleans.

interactions in the places where the mutual aid organizations are active.[19] Consciousness-raising might also include education internal to mutual aid teams: for example, training on anti-racism, disability justice, harm reduction, and gender studies.

While Southern Solidarity members in New Orleans are immersed in necessary and labor-intensive direct relief efforts that push back against decades of racist austerity measures, group members are encouraged to participate in reading groups, and training as well as protests demanding that the government provide adequate resources for all. Southern Solidarity invites the unhoused to reading groups and protests as a way to organize recipients around liberation efforts. An emancipatory mutual aid consciously strives to both prevent the further disempowerment of the recipients and, when possible, push in the other direction, providing platforms on which people can work toward determining their community's own fate.

Southern Solidarity members act under the premise that solidarity necessitates a deep understanding of the systemic forces of oppression that have created dispossession and crisis. Acts of charity alone do not require a deep understanding of systemic oppression thereby limiting their role as an integral force toward movement building. On the other hand, actionist mutual aid interventions motivated by the urge to "do something" but inattentive to contesting these hierarchies and dependencies run the risk of reestablishing exploitative relationships in the very act of trying to help out.

Practicing liberation

A mutual aid practice that aims to augment rather than reduce the autonomy and self-determination of those in need must avoid the missionary model, however secular.[20] Rather than parachuting in from the outside to save those in distress, practitioners of a liberatory mutual aid will acknowledge and work with existing community emergency response and disaster resilience networks that aren't tied into the power structure that brought about the problem in the first place.

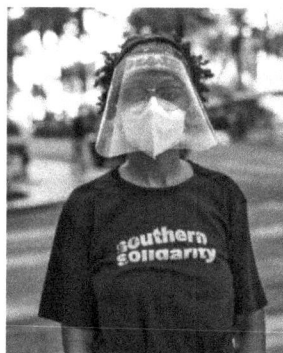

To avoid duplicating efforts already undertaken by existing organizations and to make well-informed choices about what's needed where, from the very beginning mutual aid start-ups need to break bread with other organizations in their locality. Southern Solidarity, for instance, has collaborated with a variety of organizations, including People's Assembly, Overcoming Racism, New Orleans Workers Hospitality Alliance, Trystereo, Beloved, Women with A Vision, Greater New Orleans Caring Collective, and Hidden History Tours.

In addition to connecting with local organizations, mutual aid groups with claims to radical liberatory frameworks should refer back to the work of past and current liberation fighters specific to their locale and acknowledge how people shape the current political terrain.

Despite heightened levels of inequity and racism, New Orleans, again our example, has long been a site of cultural resistance to white supremacy – what Ishmael Reed fictionalized as "Jes Grew" in the novel *Mumbo Jumbo*.[21] From the 1811 slave revolt to the recent Take 'Em Down movement, organizing in New Orleans is characterized by both the delegitimization of the narrative power of the colonial head and an emphasis on the dignity of Black life in all of its manifestations.[22] Southern Solidarity emerged out of this milieu and upholds that history by working with local healers, musicians, advocates, activists, and scholars such as Spirit McIntyre and Angela Kinlaw, who continue to pass down affirmation of Black life in a variety of ways.

Scholars with an activist impulse might be best off collaborating with community-based organizations with which they already have long-standing relations rooted in mutual trust.[23] One possible vocation of a "people's expert" is to comprehensively map community capabilities – research that enables community members themselves to better understand the array of emergency response and disaster resilience resources they already have at their disposal, as well as resources they lack. These capabilities are often grounded in distinctive histories unique to a place.[24]

For example, in the aftermath of 2018's devastating Camp Fire disaster recovery, activists in Northern California got a crash course education in disaster management policy.[25] Leveraging a core idea in the national emergency response and disaster recovery framework – the primacy of local communities in deciding the substance of disaster recovery plans – the activists coalesced around local tribal governments. The governments contended that their status as sovereign tribes qualified them as public agencies eligible to secure contracts and jobs in disaster recovery. Coalition members gained practical experience as executors of disaster recovery. The learning and skills thus acquired became part of the community's repertoire of disaster resilience capabilities, ready to be activated when the COVID-19 crisis and state lockdown directives came to Northern California.

Exercises in sizing up a community's capabilities can help community members and scholars alike realize the distinctiveness of a locality's history and conditions, and guard against the tendency to propose one-size-fits-all solutions in mutual aid practice. At the same time, a community might be endowed with remarkable survival skills, its story very much worth telling not least because there might be some generalizable lessons about disaster resilience to be drawn from it.[26] Taking an inventory of community capabilities also entails identifying social groups isolated from mainstream communication flows, such as sectarian religious groups – especially important knowledge to have on hand during contagious disease outbreaks.[27]

A bedrock principle of an emancipatory mutual aid is providing space for communities to collectively deliberate and decide upon their own needs and priorities. Assemblies and other democratic fora are settings in which such deliberation and decision-making might occur.

Consistent with this, action researchers and people's experts with an interest in emancipatory mutual aid might conceive their roles to be facilitators and catalyzers of community self-determination.

Mutual aid during COVID

The exceptional circumstances of the COVID-19 pandemic pose peculiar challenges to mutual aid organizations imbued with a self-management ethic.[28] Under ordinary circumstances, it is a rule of thumb that those who "do the work" have a prominent voice in deciding what that work will consist of, from the assessment of needs to the disbursement of funds. But when some organization members are at high risk of contracting severe COVID-19 and cannot do those aspects of "the work" that involve leaving home, there needs to be a recalibration of collective responsibilities and collective governance such that home-bound members continue to have a say in what the organization as a whole does.

Mutual aid can thus be characterized as that which is necessary to help fundamentally transform the conditions that created the crisis in the first place. The emergency was here long before the virus arrived.[29]

Mutual aid ranges from basic necessities to emotional support with the expectation that help is a shared community across giving and receiving. All must have an equal voice regardless of position or resources. Democratic organizations that are horizontal and offer opportunities for autonomous organizing offer the greatest shot at realizing the dream of the Black Panthers, the Landless Movement, and many others across the world that fed, educated, and healthy people could dismantle the capitalism and racism that, among other dangers, expose millions to the worst of outbreaks. We can bring about new worlds based on liberatory mutual aid.

14 May 2020

Pandemic Research for the People is a crowd-funded effort aimed at conducting research on questions that will directly help communities around the world during the COVID-19 pandemic. For more information or to donate to the project, please visit the PReP website: https://arerc.wordpress.com/pandemic-research-for-the-people/.

Contact. Feel free to contact PReP at https://arerc.wordpress.com/contact/ or preporganizer@gmail.com.

These dispatches are intended as provocative and informative commentary aimed at galvanizing new thinking around the present pandemic and its causes. The views in this dispatch represent those of the author/s.

References

1. Kandel N, et al. (2020) Health security capacities in the context of COVID-19 outbreak: an analysis of International Health Regulations annual report data from 182 countries. *The Lancet*, 395(10229):1047-1053; Boccia S, et al. (2020) What other countries can learn from Italy during the COVID-19 pandemic. *JAMA Internal Medicine*, 7 April. https://jamanetwork.com/journals/jamainternalmedicine/article-abstract/2764369.
2. Roberts M (2020) It was the virus that did it. Michael Roberts blog, 15 March. https://thenextrecession.wordpress.com/2020/03/15/it-was-the-virus-that-did-it/; Barua S (2020) Understanding coronanomics:

The economic implications of the coronavirus (COVID-19) pandemic (April 1, 2020). SSRN, 3 April. https://ssrn.com/abstract=3566477.

3. Wilkinson A (2020) Local response in health emergencies: key considerations for addressing the COVID-19 pandemic in informal urban settlements. *Environment and Urbanization*. https://doi. org/10.1177/0956247820922843; Acuto M (2020) COVID-19: lessons for an urban(izing) world. *One Earth*, 2(4):317-319; Beardmore A, et al. (2020). *Apart but not Alone: Neighbour Support and the Covid-19 Lockdown. Initial Findings Survey in Bristol and the West Country, 6-12 April 2020.* https://uwe- repository.worktribe.com/output/5918496/apart-but-not-alone-neighbour-support-and-the-covid-19-lockdown.

4. Newland E (2020) St. Cloud Facebook group helps share goods during coronavirus isolation. *St Cloud Times*, 18 March. https://www.sctimes.com/story/news/local/2020/03/18/st-cloud-facebook-group-helping-share-goods- during-virus-isolation/2869648001/.

5. Woo E (2020) COVID-19 and Chinese civil society's response. Stanford Social Innovation Review, 14 April. https://ssir.org/articles/entry/covid_19_and_chinese_civil_societys_response; Chen X (2020) Spaces of care and resistance in China: public engagement during the COVID-19 outbreak. *Eurasian Geography and Economics*, 8 May. https://doi.org/10.1080/15387216.2020. 1762690; Anonymous (2020) *Useful Mutual-Aid Projects in Response to COVID-19: Experience from Chinese Volunteers in Response to Coronavirus Crisis.* https://docs.google.com/document/ d/1kWBo8ff5UNz5ROWH1J1wRLA2N- WnN2JFZXmiO9ji5a8/edit?fbclid=IwAR2ch5DocCIYzBWr2N SrbviaVSSv1HdZEDC8RMm9kvkJS7pPfL_ix209t JA.

6. Saper RM (2005) *The Limits of Neoliberal Accommodation in Oaxaca's Countryside: Subsistence Debt and the Deficiencies of Self-help in a Rural Zapotec Municipality.* BA thesis, University of California, Davis. https://search.proquest.com/openview/07725ccb46d4d290ded914126bf4e4a7/1 ?pq-origsite=gscholar&cbl=18750&diss=y; Davis M (2018) Old Gods, New Enigmas: Marx's Lost Theory. Verso, New York.

7. Anonymous (2020) Autonomous groups are mobilizing mutual aid initiatives to combat the coronavirus. *It's Going Down*, 20 March. https://itsgoingdown.org/autonomous-groups-are-mobilizing-mutual-aid-initiatives- to-combat-the-coronavirus/; Brinkhurst M (2020) Creativity and compassion during COVID-19: How developers are using maps to care for their communities. Mapbox, 9 April. https://blog.mapbox.com/creativity-and- compassion-in-covid-19-ed3c0fd54c5d.

8. Anonymous (2020) COVID-19 mutual aid resources. *Big Door Brigade*, 16 March. http:// bigdoorbrigade.com/2020/03/16/covid-19-mutual-aid-resources/; Kaba M, D Spade, and A Goodman. Solidarity not charity: Mutual aid & how to organize in the age of coronavirus. Democracy Now, 20 March. https://www.democracynow.org/2020/3/20/coronavirus_community_response_mutual_aid.

9. Anonymous (2020) Who we are. Southern Solidarity https://southernsolidarity.org/about/; Flanagan A (2020) Portraits from New Orleans: A close-knit city keeping a safe distance. *New York Times,* 3 April. https://www.nytimes.com/interactive/2020/04/03/us/coronavirus-new-orleans-social-distancing.html; Gurba M (2020) Be about it: A history of mutual aid has prepared POC for this moment. *Remezcla*, 14 May. https://remezcla.com/features/culture/southern-solidarity-mutual-aid-history-and-coronavirus/.

10. Goddard N (2012) Public Housing and Gentrification in New Orleans. Amazon e-book. PreP Neighborhood / Mutual Aid Primer Dispatch 2 / Pandemic Research for the People https://www.amazon.com/Public-Housing-Gentrification-New-Orleans-ebook/dp/B078ZMW9NY; Hammer D (2020) New Orleans working to get homeless off the streets during COVID-19 crisis. WWLTV, 23 March. https://www.wwltv.com/article/news/health/coronavirus/homeless-orleans-coronavirus/289-10615f3f-a4ec- 4e0d-96c0-2194d69c31e0.

11. Kropotkin P (1902/2012) *Mutual Aid: A Factor of Evolution.* Dover Publications. Mineola, New York.

12. Anonymous (2020) Free African Society. Wikipedia. https://en.wikipedia.org/wiki/Free_African_ Society; Cambodia Mutual Assistance Association of Greater Lowell, Inc. http://www.cmaalowell.org/ wp/; Cordeiro LS, L Sibeko, and J Nelson-Peterman (2018) Healthful, cultural foods and safety net use among Cambodian and Brazilian immigrant communities in Massachusetts. *Journal of Immigrant and Minority Health*, 20:991-999.

13. Dubofsky M (1969) *We Shall Be All: A History of the Industrial Workers of the World.* Quadrangle Books; Davis M (2018) Old Gods, New Enigmas: Marx's Lost Theory.

14. Potorti M (2014) *Feeding Revolution: The Black Panther Party and the Politics of Food.* University of Pittsburgh. http://radicalteacher.library.pitt.edu/ojs/radicalteacher/article/view/80

15. Tolentino J (2020) What mutual aid can do during a pandemic. *New Yorker*, 18 May. https://www.newyorker.com/magazine/2020/05/18/what-mutual-aid-can-do-during-a-pandemic.

16. Kenney Z (2019) *Solidarity, Not Charity: Mutual Aid in Natural Disaster Relief.* Master's Thesis, Sociology, North Arizona University. https://nau.edu/wp-content/uploads/sites/83/Kenney-FINAL-Thesis.pdf.

17. Langlois J (2020) São Paulo's favelas are running out of food. These women are stepping in. *National Geographic*, 1 May. https://www.nationalgeographic.com/science/2020/05/coronavirus-brazil-sao-paulo-favelas-running-out-of-food-women-stepping-in/ .

18. Turci F (2020) Favela de São Paulo vira exemplo em ações contra o coronavírus. *Jornal Nacional,* 11 de abril, https://globoplay.globo.com/v/8476182/.

19. Spade D (2020) Solidarity not charity: Mutual aid for mobilization and survival. *Social Text,* 38(1):131-151.

20. Kenney Z (2019) *Solidarity, Not Charity: Mutual Aid in Natural Disaster Relief.*
21. Karrass GS (2019) *"The Least Sexually Confident Women in the World": International NGOs and the Racialized Politics of Obstetric Fistula NGOs and the Racialized Politics of Obstetric Fistula.* PhD Dissertation, Women's and GenderStudies, CUNY Graduate Center. https://academicworks. cuny.edu/cgi/viewcontent.cgi?article=4334&context=gc_etds.
22. Reed I (1972/1996) *Mumbo Jumbo.* Scribner, New York; Eldred N (2020) Black Mardi Gras: Resistance, resilience and the preservation of history In New Orleans. *Big Easy Magazine,* 29 February. https://www.bigeasymagazine.com/2020/02/29/black-mardi-gras-resistance-resilience-and-the-preservation-of-history-in-new-orleans/.
23. Depp B (2020) The new front line of food relief in New Orleans. New Orleans Public Radio, 11 May. https://www.wwno.org/post/new-frontline-food-relief-new-orleans.
24. Petteway R, M Mujahid, A Allen, and R Morello-Frosch (2019) Towards a people's social epidemiology: Envisioning a more inclusive and equitable future for social epi research and practice in the 21st Century. *International Journal of Environmental Research and Public Health,* 16:3983.
25. Gibson K, A Hill, and L Law (2018) Community economies in Southeast Asia : a hidden economic geography. In A McGregor, L Law, and F Miller (eds), *Routledge Handbook of Southeast Asian Development.* Routledge, Abingdon, UK, pp. 131-141.
26. Siegler K (2020) Rethinking disaster recovery after a California town is leveled by wildfire. NPR, 28 May. https://www.npr.org/2019/05/28/724404528/rethinking-disaster-recovery-after-a-california-town-is-leveled- by-wildfire.
27. Wallace D (2020) *Firefighters and EMTs in This Time of COVID-19.* Dispatch 1, Pandemic Research for the People, 5 April. https://www.facebook.com/PandemicResearchForThePeople/photos/pcb.1211 14749531735/121112942865249/?type=3&theater.
28. Clare S (2019) Building social capital to increase disaster resilience. In PE Perkins (ed) *Local Activism for Global Climate Justice: The Great Lakes Watershed.* Routledge, Abingdon, UK pp. 158-165; Kenney Z (2019) *Solidarity, Not Charity: Mutual Aid in Natural Disaster Relief.*
29. Pickerill J and Paul Chatterton (2006) Notes towards autonomous geographies: creation, resistance and self- management as survival tactics. *Progress in Human Geography,* 30(6):730-746; Ince A (2015) From middle ground to common ground: Self-management and spaces of encounter in organic farming networks. *Annals of the Association of American Geographers,* 105(4):824-840.
30. Baker PC (2020) 'We can't go back to normal': how will coronavirus change the world? *The Guardian,* 31 March. https://www.theguardian.com/world/2020/mar/31/how-will-the-world-emerge-from-the-coronavirus-crisis.

Can agroecology stop COVID-21, -22, and -23?

MOVING BEYOND CAPITALIST AGRICULTURE

*Alexander Liebman,[a] Tammi Jonas,[b,c] Ivette Perfecto,[d] Lisa Kelley,[e]
Henry Anton Peller,[f] Salvatore Engel-Dimauro,[g] Kevon Rhiney,[h]
Philip Seufert,[i] Luis Fernando Chaves,[j] Luke Bergmann,[k]
Kim Williams-Guillén,[l,m] Max Ajl,[n] Etant Dupain,[o] John Gulick,[o]
and Rob Wallace[o]*

PReP Agroecologies

COVID-19 has circled the planet several times the first year into the outbreak, reshaping nearly all aspects of human society.

It's now clear that the virus worsens the underlying forms of violence that capitalism imposes upon everyday people. Unemployment remains through the roof. Public health is damaged beyond the outbreak itself, with, for instance, riskier childbirths and failing campaigns in malaria elimination.[1] In contrast, massive public bailouts are being handed over to the more politically connected industrial sectors, including, in the U.S., fracking companies, cruise ships, and airlines, as exploited frontline workers and whole communities go uninsured and unprotected.[2] We see the impacts in the rise of racist, fascist rhetoric broadcast across countries. From street vigilantes to neoliberal and authoritarian governments, the coronavirus is painted as an exotic aberration originating in "other" people.

Caricatures of Chinese peasants, meatpacking workers, Black and Latinx communities, and immigrants have been ramped up into outright violence.[3] There are liberal versions too, finger wagging at "covidiots," from Hassidic wedding parties in Brooklyn to open taprooms worldwide. At odds with the line we are often handed by politicians and leaders that we are all in this together, it could not be clearer that Black, Brown, and

a PhD student, Department of Geography, Rutgers University, **b** Farmer, Jonai Farms & Meatsmiths, **c** President, Australian Food Sovereignty Alliance, **d** Professor, School for Environment and Sustainability, University of Michigan, **e** Assistant Professor, Geography and Environmental Sciences, University of Colorado, Denver, **f** Doctoral candidate, School of Environment and Natural Resources, The Ohio State University, **g** Associate Professor, Department of Geography, SUNY New Paltz, **h** Assistant Professor, Department of Geography, Rutgers University, **i** Programme Coordinator, FIAN International, **j** Disease ecologist and International Coordinator, Agroecology and Rural Economics Research Corps, **k** Department of Geography, University of British Columbia, **l** Farmer, Flight Path Farms **m** Adjunct Assistant, Ecosystem Science and Management, University of Michigan, **n** Researcher, Tunisian Observatory for Food Sovereignty and the Environment, **o** Organizer, Pandemic Research for the People

Indigenous communities are disproportionately suffering the effects of COVID-19.[4] On the other hand, denialism about the disease among the likes of Trumpists in the U.S. and Bolsonaristas in Brazil is intensifying a decades-long abandonment of the public commons as concept and practice. The pandemic continues the already ongoing damage that racialized groups – deprived of societal resources because of their skin color alone – suffer from racial, climate, and environmental injustices often interacting together.

These injustices aren't just reflected in the pandemic's damage. They are also the outbreak's cause. Pathogens repeatedly are emerging out of a global agrifood system rooted in inequality, labor exploitation, and unfettered extractivism by which communities are robbed of their natural and social resources. A crisis-prone economic system that prioritizes production for profit over meeting human needs and ecological preservation is organized around the intense monocultural production that, along the way, allows the deadliest of diseases to emerge.

The PReP Agroecologies working group we're introducing here with this dispatch will be focusing on how agriculture might be reimagined as the kind of community-wide intervention that could stop coronaviruses and other pathogens from emerging in the first place. That's a critical program wherever we live – in an agricultural community or in the center of a city. In later dispatches, we'll be describing how such an effort might work. But for this first dispatch, we will push back against the way the injustices of the present food system are reproduced in the basic science upon which we depend to make decisions about that system. Then we will give an overview of agroecology as a revolutionary pathway to move beyond capitalist industrial agriculture.

In the USA and elsewhere, liberal politicians, including the Biden administration, are appealing to science as our ticket out of the COVID trap.[5] But what kind of science? And is the science chosen going to do the job? What exactly is that job and for whom is it pursued? In this dispatch, we address how mainstream science is helping power the political and economic systems that helped produce the pandemic.

Specifically, we work through how recent analyses of the connections among urbanization, industry, and agriculture have been used to argue for more of the kinds of surveillance and population displacement that help bring about many of the world's current crises, this time "updated" in the name of controlling disease. Our commentary details a recent high-profile report by global change ecologist Rory Gibb and his colleagues in

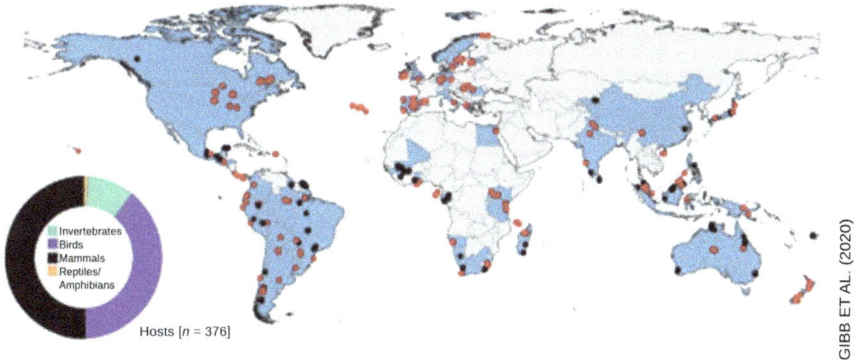

The PREDICTS dataset (footnote 6) is a global collection of the relationship between land use and zoonotic host types. Mammal survey locations are in black, surveys for other taxa in red, and nations sampled in blue (n=6,801 sites). The data set is useful in drawing general hypotheses across land-use change, the restructuring of ecological communities, and disease emergence. However, PrEP Agroecologies is wary of conclusions drawn from this data set that target specific forms of agriculture, rural livelihoods, and regions for increased surveillance and regulation. Without combining these forms of meta-analyses with local data, a fine-grained understanding of how land-use change is impacted by extractivism, and a differentiation of various forms of agriculture and settlement, the conclusions derived from the data are inevitably draconian and based upon existing Euro-centric forms of environmental governance. Graphic adapted from Gibb et al. (2020).

Nature on the interconnection between land-use change, biodiversity, and zoonotic diseases – diseases that emerge out of nonhuman animals.[6]

We highlight the importance of the group's findings while also pointing out the perils of the way in which this work has been mapped onto policy and intervention. If followed through, the expectations and conclusions of the Gibb group are likely to further reproduce the very kinds of social and ecological damage that the study supposedly addresses.

We finish up here by introducing agroecology, an environmentalism of the peasantry, the poor, and indigenous, long in practice, that treats agriculture as a part of the ecology out of which humanity grows its food. We present the approach as both a pathway forward for the world and as an alternative that folds in the insights of the Gibb study without falling into the worst of its traps.

Disease emergence and land-use drivers

Zoonotic diseases like COVID-19 are caused by pathogens that circulate in nonhuman reservoirs – bats, apes, birds, and other animals – before spilling over into human populations. The initial transmission often occurs in forested regions where animals that host the pathogens first come into contact with humans. Local forest and fisher folk are part of what are porous ecological communities shared by humans and nonhumans alike, and have been for thousands of years. As forests become increasingly destroyed, fragmented, homogenized, and stressed, scientists have documented an increase in the incidence of disease outbreaks.[7] Forested areas are split up and transformed into cities small and large, industrial areas, or large plantations; as a result, animal-human interactions go through fundamental changes. Occasional contact between human populations and animal disease hosts turns more frequent due to the cascading social, economic, and ecological changes that occur at the forest frontier.

The Gibb study documents the ways in which land-use changes, however narrowly the team defines them, not only increase the prevalence of zoonotic diseases but also change the composition of disease hosts. Humanity is increasingly opened up to greater pathogen exposure. More specifically, the Gibb team provides important empirical documentation of a long-theorized relation: that landscapes altered by human activity, especially agriculture and urbanization, vaguely defined categories here, decrease the animal diversity that blocks pathogens from easily lining up a string of transmission out of the forest.[8]

Gibb and colleagues draw on a unique dataset called PREDICTS, which synthesizes information from hundreds of biodiversity and land-use change studies conducted across the world.[9] The team uses the dataset to illuminate the kinds of broad comparisons in environments across the planet that were previously elusive. In doing so, the team documents how the encroachment upon forest edges leads to more contact and exposure between humans and animals producing spillover events. However, land-use change also transforms the composition of animal communities, with the remaining animal species often representing more effective viral hosts.

The problem with the Gibb report is not in these findings, which are an excellent contribution, but in how the authors use their findings to support simplistic policy conclusions that play into the hands of the powerful who brought about the environmental damage driving the new outbreaks in the first place. Specifically, the authors advocate a series of punitive interventions. They call for an increase in forest surveillance and flat-out excluding humans living in the forest, many for thousands of years, all in an effort to limit deforestation and the compounding ecological damage. The team proposes increased funding for international conventions in regulating wildlife trade and biodiversity. In doing so, they join a series of other high-profile calls for such measures, including one published in the journal *Science*.[10] Addressing deforestation is no simple task, yet these exercises in top-down environmental governance further strip peasants, smallholders, and working-class rural people of their right to manage the landscapes in which they live.

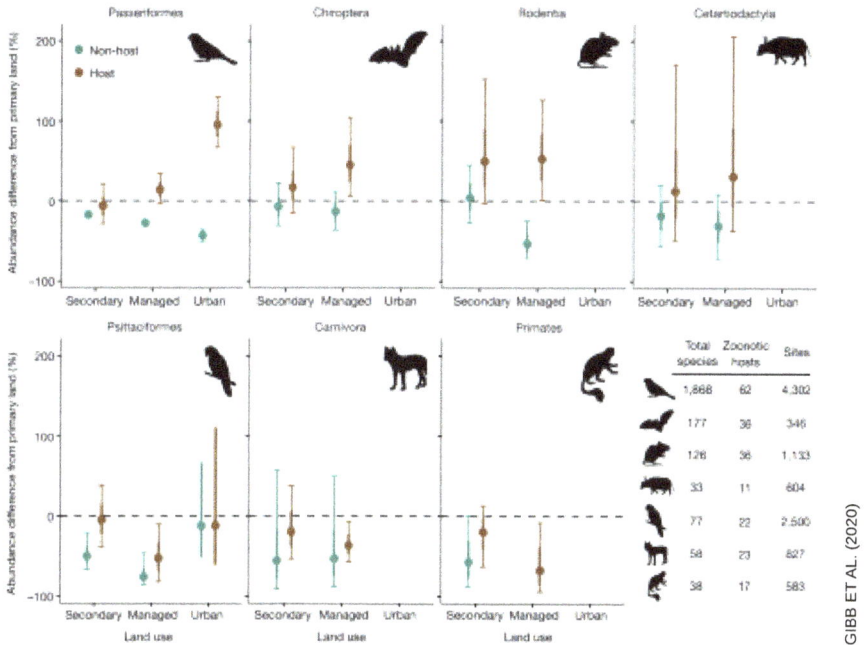

Increasing human encroachment led to an increasing proportion of species able to host pathogens that infect humans. Those species that tended to be non-hosts disappeared from the landscape. Here, the team shows such differences by specific host taxa, especially, across the top, for song birds, bats, rodents, and even-toed ungulates. Along the X-axis are three forms of land-use change – secondary forest (secondary), agriculture (managed) and urban. Along the Y-axis the percent change in abundance of the species from primary land that has not undergone pervasive transformation. For example, for the order Passeriformes (a ubiquitous order, containing about ½ of all bird species), zoonotic disease hosts increase in managed and urban landscapes, while non-host species decline. Graphic adapted from Gibb et al. (2020).

Enclosure – violently pushing peasants off the land and coercing them into working on large-scale plantations – is a defining component of capitalism back to its earliest days. Capital since has searched the world for new landscapes and labor pools from which to extract value.[11] Under the guise of sustainability and disease control, capital, and the science long in its pay, is now pivoting toward taking advantage of disease crises of its own making. Land grabbing, stealing land from Indigenous people and smallholders, is pursued in the name of conservation and, suddenly, preventing pandemics.

So, agricultural expansion into the forest frontier is not driven by "farmers,""smallholders," or "peasants." Rather, extractive development – including agro-industrialization, logging, and mining – financializing commodity production on the global market, and supply chain consolidation have enabled unprecedented multinational growth into forested lands over the past three decades.[12]

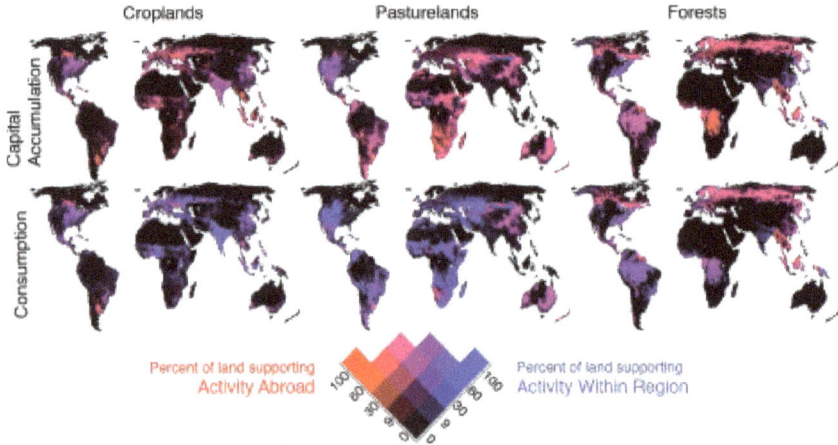

There are other ways of conducting land-use analyses. This study uses Eckert IV projects to demonstrate how land uses such as cropland, pastureland, and forest are influenced by capital accumulation (top row) and consumption (bottom row) within region and abroad (Bergmann L and M Holmberg (2016) Land in motion. *Annals of the American Association of Geographers* 106(4) 932-956.). The important takeaway here is the level to which capital flows drive land-use change designated for export-oriented commodity production. For example, in the case of W. Africa above, croplands are almost 100 percent (bright pink) devoted for production abroad. This type of data helps to conceptualize how local drivers of zoonotic viruses through land-use change are frequently the outcome of responses to global investments in agriculture. Environmental impacts aren't merely matters of damage at the GPS coordinates of interest, an approach that places undue focus on local peoples and their practices. Here capital and consumption flow in what are called relational geographies. What happens on one side of the world can impact landscapes on the other. The approach places focus on how power is exercised far from the initial locales out of which, in this case, new diseases emerge.

These dynamics not only transform local ecologies; they also displace local inhabitants. Displacement isn't just about a locale. Displacement includes separating peoples from their way of life. Multinational plantations, for instance, play workers off one another by recruiting more exploitable people, a practice dating back to slavery days when indentured Indian laborers were brought in to supplement labor shortages on sugar plantations in the Caribbean. In upending existing communities this way, large plantations also help spread pathogens. Many zoonotic diseases are emerging right out of commodity production.

Whereas a farmer might have tended to a small herd of cattle at a forest clearing and sold these animals in towns nearby, international investments in agriculture transform the same land into intensive livestock or crop production, bringing in laborers from across the countryside to disease focal points in the forest and then shipping out the foods produced, including live animals carrying pathogens, over thousands of kilometers. Lengthening labor and commodity chains shotguns out the emergent diseases when previously the pathogens were bottled up in local dynamics.

The expansion of monoculture plantations such as oil palm in West Africa kicked out local forest farmers, producing ideal conditions for the proliferation of bats, primary vectors for a variety of zoonotic viruses, leading to what was at that time the largest documented Ebola outbreak in 2013-2015.[13] With competitors and predators stripped out, several bat species migrated into such plantations, expanding their interfaces with the migratory labor working the fields.

Displaced peasants do not disappear. Some may depend more heavily on (now commonly condemned) sources of wild protein within remnant forests, with bushmeat – more a commodity than the subsistence food it once was – acting as another source of infection. Many local laborers are often forced to work in urban industrial centers during the off-season, carrying diseases from forest edges to urban centers and back again.[14]

Indeed, the story of smallholder displacement and labor mobility now appears central to the intertwined political economy and ecology of land use, rural livelihoods, and zoonotic disease. This much is apparent

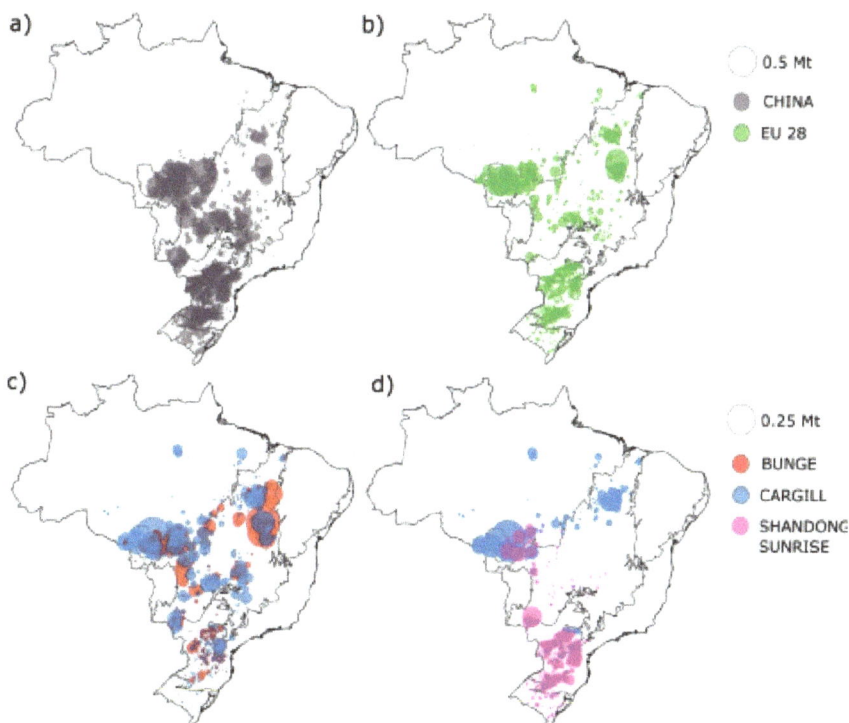

The spatial origins of soy production in Brazil based on trade data in metric tons. The gray (a) shows the tonnage and spatial origins of what is consumed by China. The green (b) is what is consumed by the European Union. Bottom left (c) depicts soy tonnage exported out of Brazil by two U.S. agribusiness corporations, Cargill and Bunge. Bottom right (d) depicts soy imported by Cargill and Shandong Sunrise, and then either exported through secondary shipping subsidiaries or used in domestic feed supplies. In both c) and d), Cargill (blue) is at the forefront of destroying primary forest in the Amazon. Godar J, C Suavet, TA Gardner, E Dawkins and P Meyfroidt (2016) Balancing detail and scale in assessing transparency to improve the governance of agricultural commodity supply chains. *Environmental Research Letters* 11: 035015 from the disproportionate COVID-19 fatalities being borne by migrant populations in one of the wealthiest nations of the world, Singapore, a country that depends on migrant laborers, many of whom long displaced from their agrarian communities.[15] COVID-19 has ravaged migrant Latinx agricultural workers in California's Central Valley, with a disproportionate number of migrant workers living in substandard housing, sparking xenophobic attacks.[16] In Costa Rica, authorities have deployed surveillance drones to monitor Nicaraguan migrants in the name of COVID.[17] The Gibb team's calls for sterilizing the forest are in reality embodied by these kinds of operations, turning life along these "neoliberal frontiers" into an archipelago of prisons and work camps.[18]

Agroecological approaches to preventing disease

Gibb's team also falls into a pattern almost ubiquitous across conservation biology and disease ecology when discussing the effects of agriculture on land use. By relying on the very large but non-specific PREDICTS database, the authors clump agriculture into one of four land use classes – primary vegetation, nearby secondary vegetation, managed lands, and urban space, which are further subdivided into two intensities based on use: minimal and substantial. The managed category bundles cropland, pasture, and plantation into a single agriculture designation.

Aside from the analytical limits in lumping together a wide diversity of production systems, the approach boxes out very real, material consequences, making them at one and the same time invisible and, for the powerful, governable. The crude divisions omit many forms of peasant, indigenous, and smallholder agriculture methods that are integrated within forest ecosystems and produce food and fiber for local and regional uses while preserving high levels of agrobiodiversity and wildlife diversity.[19]

In the other direction, agricultural intensification under the guise of sparing "wilderness" can lead to greater deforestation and disease spillover. By the *Jevons paradox*, more efficient extraction and cheapening production can increase resource use and associated environmental destruction overall.[20] Empirical evidence suggests that, with few exceptions, agricultural intensification programs lead to more deforestation, not less.[21] So the specific mode of agriculture matters a great deal in assessing its role in forest destruction, biodiversity loss, and the production of food.[22] All this is missed by relying on massive databases divorced from the lives of agriculturalists living in the forest regions under consideration.

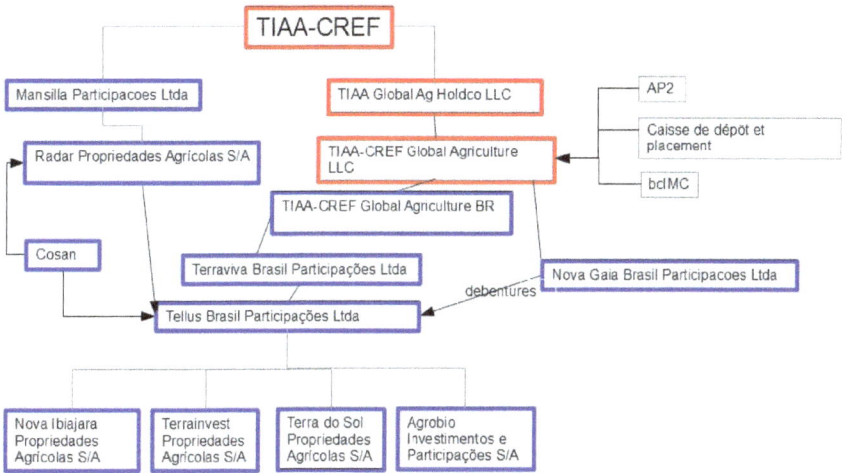

REDE SOCIAL DE JUSTIÇA E DIREITOS HUMANOS ET AL. 2015

It isn't just agricultural multinationals. TIAA, which handles the retirement funds of many U.S. universities, also organizes farmland investments in Brazil through U.S.-based funds in the red and Brazilian ones in blue. The pension fund is investing hundreds of millions into Brazilian fund Radar Propriedades Agrícolas, co-created with giant sugar producer Cosan to acquire land for sugarcane and other commodity crops. Cosan manages the fund. By 2012, Radar acquired 392 farms in Brazil of over 150,000 hectares of an estimated value over 1 billion U.S. dollars. TIAA invests into Brazilian farmland by a second pathway: TIAA-CREF Global Agriculture is a $2 billion global farmland fund aimed at Australia, Brazil, and the U.S. To circumvent Brazilian law against foreign acquisitions, this farmland fund invests indirectly through Tellus Brasil Participações, also managed by Cosan.

The type of agriculture and livestock production can act as a critical factor in driving livestock, crop, and human diseases.[23] Growing vast monocultures removes any immunogenetic diversity that might cut off disease transmission. In industrial animal production, the densely packed barns, housing as many as 250,000 birds and supplying feed full of antibiotics, simultaneously increase the possibility of disease transmission and depress immune response. Raising animals as fast as possible, while continually re-populating farms with new batches of nearly genetically identical animals, creates a constantly renewed supply of susceptible hosts that rewards the deadliest strains. Growing out food at such concentrations rewards those pathogen strains that can burn through crops and food animals fastest.

Reproduction happens in labs far away from the farm, selecting for point-of-sale characteristics such as fast growth and bigger breast meat. By this breeding, natural selection favoring immunity is removed as an ecosystem service that nature provides everyday nearly for free. Along the way, even our medicines are failing. Public health is damaged when widespread use of antibiotics selects for drug resistance in livestock and human populations.[24] Industrial agriculture breeds pest and pathogen deadliness as a cost of cheap food, a cost not paid by the companies pursuing such production.

Agroeclogical principles for the design of biodiverse, energy efficient, resource-conserving and resilient farming systems

• **Enhance the recycling of biomass**, with a view to optimizing organic matter decomposition and nutrient cycling over time.

• **Strengthen the "immune system" of agricultural systems** through enhancement of functional biodiversity – natural enemies, antagonists, etc.

• **Provide the most favorable soil conditions** for plant growth, particularly by managing organic matter and by enhancing soil biological activity.

• **Minimize losses of energy, water, nutrients and genetic resources** by enhancing conservatiuon and regeneration of soil and water resources and agrobiodiversity.

• **Diversify species and genetic resources** in the agroecosystem over time and space at the field and landscape level.

• **Enhance beneficial biological interactions and synergies** among the components of agrobiodiversity, thereby promoting key ecological processes and services.

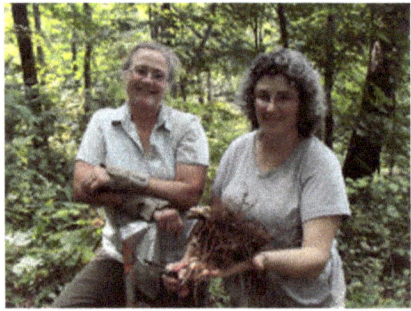

PHOTOS: ALEX LIEBMAN (TOP LEFT), KEVON RHINEY (BOTTOM LEFT), AND JODI HELMER (BOTTOM RIGHT)

Peasant agroecologies integrate community control and ecological complexity, both of which support local population health, fundamental on its own terms, but also boxing out circulating pathogens from the global travel network. Top left: Agroecology-in-practice at the IALA Maria Cano agroecology school in Viotá, Colombia, a political agroecology pedagogy center supported by FENSUAGRO (the Colombian national agricultural union) and an in-country site of La Via Campesina, the global peasant organization. Top right: table of agroecological principles as presented by Miguel Altieri and colleagues (2012). Lower left: shade-grown coffee in the Jamaican Blue Mountains. Lower right: Members of the Appalachian Beginning Forest Farmer Coalition (ABFFC) in the U.S. https://foodfirst.org/wp-content/uploads/2014/06/JA11-The-Scaling-Up-of-Agroecology-Altieri.pdf. Helmer J (2020) "In Appalachia, Forest Farming is Protecting Wild Botanical Plants" Civil Eats. https://civileats.com/2020/02/19/in-appalachia-forest-farming-is-protecting-wild-botanical-plants/

There is a way out of such a planned mess. Agroecology – a science, movement, and practice – combines ecological science, indigenous and peasant knowledges, and social movements for food and territorial sovereignty to actualize environmentally just food systems.[25] To date, there have been few efforts examining how agroecology might address the increasing proliferation of zoonotic pathogens in the world today – a world rapidly reshaped by global warming and the fragmentation of people and landscapes cut up by hypermobile capital.

We propose that peasant- and indigenous-led agroecology is uniquely positioned to limit the spread of zoonotic viruses:

Peasant agroecology champions the Indigenous and smallholders who protect agricultural biodiversity. A diverse agroecological matrix of farm plots, agroforestry, and grazing lands all embedded within a forest can conserve animal biodiversity in the landscape. Agricultural biodiversity can make it more difficult for zoonotic diseases to prevail. Such a mode of conservation also takes into account the economic and social conditions of people currently tending the land, rather than a conservation that uproots people.[26]

Large-scale growers operating in competitive global commodity markets prioritize profits over conservation. With people evacuated from surrounding forests, there may be little to stop large-scale plantations and agribusiness from expanding, disregarding conservation promises or policy mandates.[27] Such land grabs further degrade biodiversity, amplifying disease outbreaks. Alongside the racist and classist enclosure upon which intensification-as-conservation is predicated, such a program fails to meet its own declared objectives.

In contrast, integrating ecological management and the politics of equitable access to resources has long been a core focus of agroecology.[28] Such a system protects the kinds of mosaic landscapes that, by their diversity and complexity alone, lock in the deadliest pathogens from escaping out to the greater world.

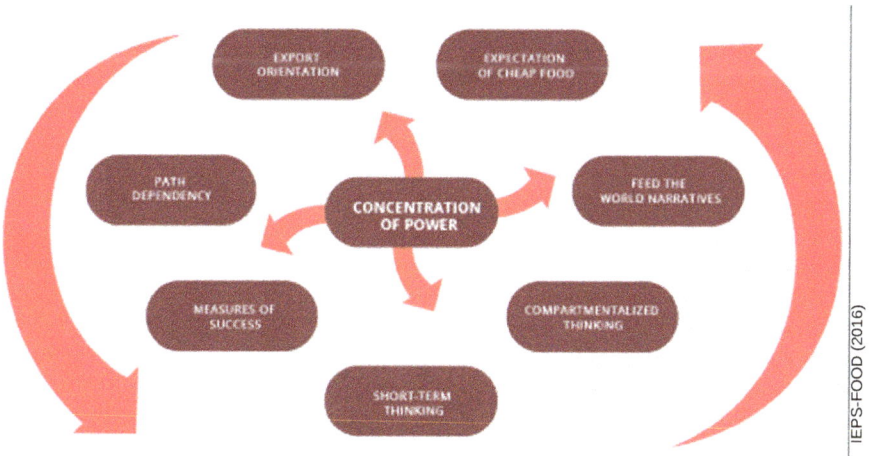

Industrial agribusiness is embodied by a network of social lock-ins that positively reinforce each other: feed the-world narratives, compartmentalized thinking, export economics, and the like (IPES Food (2016) From uniformity to diversity: a paradigm shift from industrial agriculture to diversified agroecological systems. International Panel of Experts on Sustainable Food Systems. http://www. ipes-food.org/_img/upload/files/UniformityToDiversity_FULL.pdf). Value accrues, according to the International Panel of Experts on Sustainable Food Systems (IPES) (2016), to "a limited number of actors, reinforcing their economic and political power, and thus their ability to influence the governance of food systems."

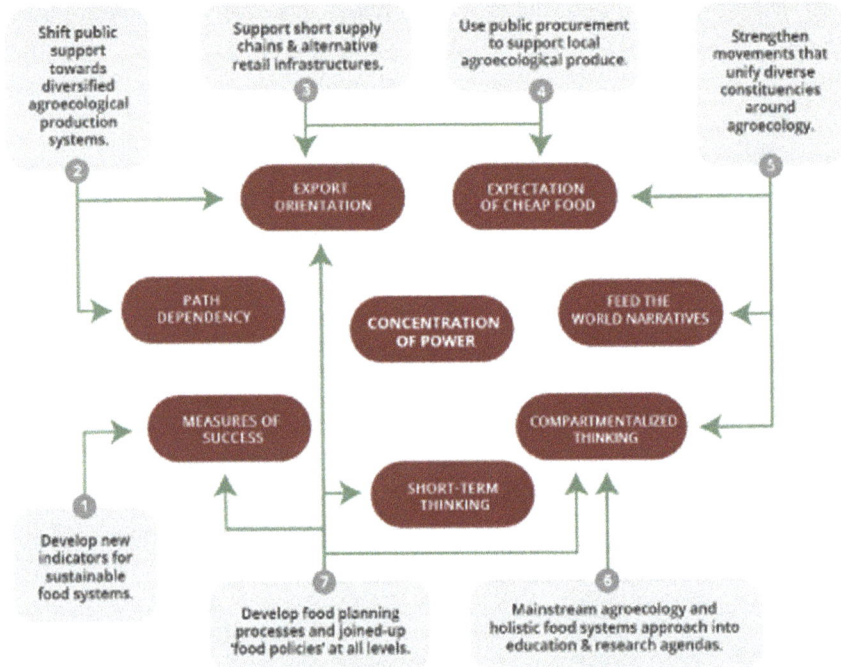

IPES proposes one way out of the agribusiness trap, recommending a series of interventions that unlock the vicious cycles out of industrial agriculture's favor: So, for instance, "Develop new indicators for sustainable food systems" and "Shift public support toward diversified agroecological production systems" and so on. These actions intervene in each of part of the vicious cycle and link the interventions into a new virtuous cycle.

Peasant agroecology folds in food sovereignty from the start. Agroecology is attuned to the ways the dynamics of settler colonialism, financializing nature, and imbalances in political power limit access to sufficient land and resources for the rural poor.[29] Inadequate access to land, industrial agricultural intensification, and exclusion from markets have been identified as socio-ecological drivers that force peasant farmers to adopt practices that lower agricultural productivity and reduce biodiversity.[30]

Alternatively, food sovereignty and agroecology programs emphasize protecting the viability of a diverse landscape that supports rural livelihoods while maintaining biodiversity. These benefits counteract neoliberal policies that focus on conventional agricultural intensification aimed at producing export-oriented cash crops and that put smallholders in a disadvantageous economic environment. Absence of agroecological movements and policies frequently push smallholders to the margins of agricultural work.

Pressures to participate in competitive markets often influence smallholders' decisions to shorten fallow periods and expand production into forests and onto hillsides, practices that can reduce ecological depth and jeopardize income opportunities. Longer fallow periods allow the development of older secondary forests that can store more carbon, improving the nutrient content of soils while enhancing habitat for wildlife and maintaining biodiversity of the landscape.[31] These same forests also provide more abundant and higher quality forest products for rural smallholders.[32]

Agroecological production practices depend on more than merely sufficient land access but, in addition, stable, equitable land tenure. Land justice is at the root of social and environmental justice. Without such justice, smallholders often must intensify production for market sale instead of their own subsistence, along the way driving the prices they earn at the market downward.[33] Despite growing more under these conditions, smallholders may unwittingly be forced into producing the conditions for increased food insecurity. Interlinking farmer livelihoods, stable and equitable land tenure, and biodiverse, forest-agriculture landscapes helps resolve age-old agrarian crises and disease spillover events in rural and wilder areas.

Peasant agroecology produces geographic mosaics that stymie the deadliest of pathogens. By prioritizing ecological management of crop and animal production and their pathogens, agroecology is likely – in a reverse of what the Gibb group documents – to decrease disease vectors. Crop

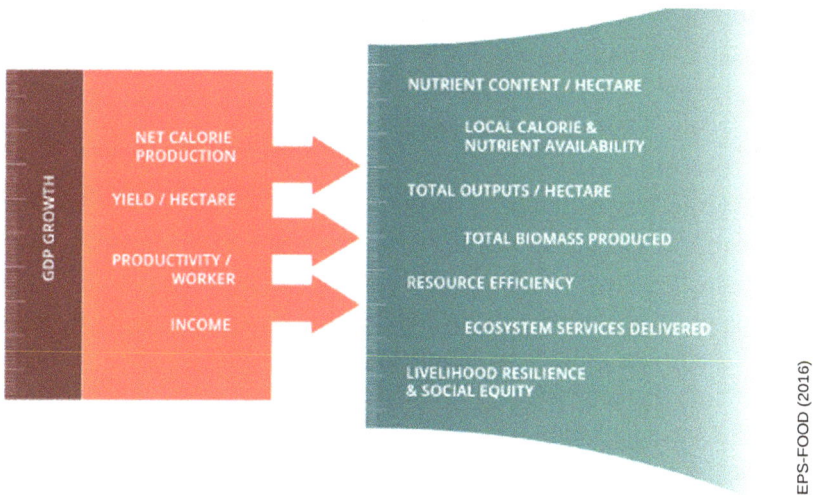

Reorganizing agriculture around different values, IPES continues, leads to replacing standard markers of agricultural production with measures of community and ecological well-being. Instead of net calorie production or yield per hectare, for instance, we can measure nutrient content per hectare, nutrient availability for local communities, livelihood resilience, and social and health equity.

genetic diversity reduces the spread of plant pathogens and acts as a core intervention in crop disease management practices.[34] The effects of livestock species' genetic diversity on zoonotic disease have been less studied and require more research.[35]

Peasant agroecology buffers against pathogen escape. The production of food and fiber for local and regional contexts slows the kinds of circulation of goods and people that accelerate disease trajectories well beyond their local origins. Building on the scenarios detailed above, regional trade reduces the spatial extent of livestock movement, greatly reducing the speed of transmission and the expanse over which pathogens can recombine their genes to deadlier effect. But disease ecologies depend on more than just spatial extent. Farmer livelihoods that are dignified and rooted in the material well-being of people and their environments are far different from the livelihood activities that require large-scale migration to cramped, poorly constructed quarters. All work is not created equal, and some work drastically increases the risk of disease transmission and exposure. Delinking viral evolution and population health from the expanding circuits of capital and labor is a key point of intervention moving forward.

Peasant agroecology addresses the disease ecologies that rural areas and cities share. While agroecology has long focused on rural areas, the approach also has shifted to urban food production and agrarian livelihoods in cities and where the rural and urban meet. Food production and access constitute a wide range of human experiences. Agroecological approaches to human and nonhuman health that prioritize landscape planning, anti-racist and anti-sexist organizing, combining households with social shared spaces (the "commons"), and environmental justice are addressing zoonotic disease management in urban spaces as well. Not all modes of urbanization (including agriculture) are the same. Concrete steps can be taken to link access to housing and land use with disease management in ways that expand human dignity and well-being rather than limiting them. Adequate housing equipped with waste removal and anti-vector architecture reduces transmission possibilities for disease pathogens. This scenario is far different from current policies, including private COVID testing and proprietary vaccines for the global elite, on the one hand, and live-and-let-die public policies for the rest.[36]

Agroecological solutions are social in origin. Limiting zoonotic disease requires committed, long term research that explores the relationships among rural livelihoods, global supply chains, and public health.

Agriculture isn't just about healthy soils and carbon sequestration. As practitioners at Soul Fire Farm in New York State (www.soulfirefarm.org) here embody and practice, food is a social system. The natural economy of agriculture can be maintained only when connected to farmer autonomy, community socioeconomic resilience, circular economies, land trusts, integrated cooperative supply networks, food justice, reparations, and reversing deeply historical race, class, and gender trauma. Healing the metabolic rift between ecology and economy driving climate damage and disease emergence at the heart of modern agriculture involves imprinting a different political philosophy upon the landscape.

Research should happen in conjunction with place-based, grassroots projects of mutual aid, food provisioning, and political mobilizations that have supported life in the face of disintegrating (if not actively genocidal) governance, climate shocks, and widening economic inequalities.

Peasant agroecologies are more than matters of soil and food, as important as those are. Agroecologies require practical politics that place agency and power in the hands of poor and working class, Indigenous, and Black and brown people. These practices replace the dynamics of ecologically harmful urbanization and agricultural industrialization operating in favor of racial and patriarchal capitalism. Agroecologies put planet and people before profits that benefit only the few.

An Invitation

Should the worst of conditions persist and deepen in the coming months, years, and decades, smallholders will remain on the frontlines of both providing food and controlling disease. As they have for centuries, those with the autonomy to exercise community control will continue to aim at maintaining biodiverse ecosystems that provide sustenance outside pathological commodity logics. These adaptive forms of resistance-as-survival – seed-saving, nutrient cycling, regional trade, and cultural, social, and philosophical ties to land – have persisted in the face of colonial, neocolonial, and now neoliberal attempts to erase them.

Indeed, the current complex of COVID-induced crises fits hand-in-glove with the system's "normal" operation. Stability has been the delusional realm of a small sliver of the Global North, awash in post-World War Two imperialism and the repeated reinvention (and re-imposition) of various plantation systems of cheap and racialized labor.

A deadly global pandemic has cracked the stable mirage, even if only partially. As most of us write from inside the Global North, we see this moment as an opportunity to articulate a liberatory politics that combats the ongoing mutilation of bodies and nature that racial capitalism imposes. For us, agroecology lies at the center of any political process resolving the dual destruction of nature and people, from which COVID hatched.

We invite anyone interested in such efforts to pitch in their ideas and practices to PReP Agroecologies. We would love to hear from you.

December 10, 2020

Pandemic Research for the People is a crowd-funded effort aimed at conducting research on questions that will directly help communities around the world during the ongoing COVID-19 pandemic. For more information or to donate to the project, please visit the PReP website: https://www.prepthepeople.net/.

Contact. Feel free to contact PReP Agroecologies at aml419@scarletmail. rutgers.edu or preporganizer@gmail.com.

These dispatches are intended as provocative and informative commentary aimed at galvanizing new thinking around the present pandemic and its causes. The views in this dispatch represent those of the authors and not necessarily that of Pandemic Research for the People.

References

1. Roberton T, et al. (2020) Early estimates of the indirect effects of the COVID-19 pandemic on maternal and child mortality in low-income and middle-income countries: a modelling study. *The Lancet,* 8(7):901-908; Weiss DJ, et al. (2020) Indirect effects of the COVID-19 pandemic on malaria intervention coverage, morbidity, and mortality in Africa: a geospatial modelling analysis. *The Lancet.* https://doi.org/10.1016/S1473-3099(20)30700-3.
2. Brenner R (2020), Escalating plunder. *New Left Review,* 123:5–22.
3. Trilling D (2020) Migrants aren't spreading coronavirus – but nationalists are blaming them anyway. *The Guardian,* 28 February. https://www.theguardian.com/commentisfree/2020/feb/28/coronavirus-outbreak migrants-blamed-italy-matteo-salvini-marine-le-pen; Gover AR, SB Harper, and L Langton (2020) Anti-Asian hate crime during the COVID-19 pandemic: Exploring the reproduction of inequality. *American Journal of Criminal Justice,* 45:647-667; Gao G and L Sai (2020) Opposing the toxic apartheid: The painted veil of the COVID-19 pandemic, race and racism. *Gender, Work & Organization.* https://doi.org/10.1111/gwao.12523; Roberto KJ, AF Johnson, and BM Rauhaus (2020) Stigmatization and prejudice during the COVID-19 pandemic. *Administrative Theory & Praxis,* 42(3):364-378; Wallace RG (2020) The kill floor. In RG Wallace, *Dead Epidemiologists: On the Origins of COVID-19.* Monthly Review Press, pp 64-77.
4. Laster Pirtle WN. (2020) Racial capitalism: A fundamental cause of novel coronavirus (COVID-19) pandemic inequities in the United States. *Health Education & Behavior,* 47(4):504-508.

5. Wallace RG (2020) Biden's COVID plan is better than Trump's, but still far from sufficient. *Truthout,* November 22. https://truthout.org/articles/bidens-covid-plan-is-better-than-trumps-but-still-far-from-sufficient/.
6. Gibb R, et al. (2020) Zoonotic host diversity increases in human-dominated ecosystems. *Nature,* 584:398-402.
7. Celli A (1933) *The History of Malaria in the Roman Campagna from Ancient Times.* John Bale, Sons & Danielsson, Ltd., London; Levins R, et al. (1994) The emergence of new diseases. *American Scientist,* 82(1):52-60; Brock PM, et al. (2019) Predictive analysis across spatial scales links zoonotic malaria to deforestation. *Proceedings of the Royal Society B,* 286(1894):20182351; Rohr, J.R., et al. (2019) Emerging human infectious diseases and the links to global food production. *Nature Sustainability,* 2(6):445-456.
8. Wallace R, LF Chaves, LR Bergmann, C Ayres, L Hogerwerf, R Kock, and RG Wallace (2018) *Clear-Cutting Disease Control: Capital-Led Deforestation, Public Health Austerity, and Vector-Borne Infection.* Springer, Cham.
9. Hudson LN, et al. (2017). The database of the PREDICTS (Projecting Responses of Ecological Diversity In Changing Terrestrial Systems) Project. *Ecology and Evolution,* 7(1):145-188.
10 Dobson AP, et al. (2020) Ecology and economics for pandemic prevention. *Science,* 369(6502): 379-381.
11. Marx K (1977) *Capital: Volume 1.* trans. Ben Fowkes. Penguin Books, New York; Amin S (1990) *Delinking: Towards a Polycentric World.* Zed Books, London; Luxembourg R (2003) *The Accumulation of Capital.* Routledge Classics, London; Suwandi I (2019) *Value Chains: The New Economic Imperialism.* Monthly Review Press, New York.
12. Vásquez-Leon M and D Liverman (2004) The political ecology of land-use change: Affluent ranchers and destitute farmers in the Mexican municipio of Alamos. *Human Organization,* 63:21-33; Zoomers A (2010) Globalization and the foreignization of space: seven processes driving the current global land grab. *Journal of Peasant Studies,* 37(2):429-447; Hecht SB and A Cockburn (2011) *The Fate of the Forest.* University of Chicago Press, Chicago; McMichael P (2012) The land grab and corporate food regime restructuring. *Journal of Peasant Studies,* 39:681- 701; Borras Jr SM, C Kay, S Gómez and J Wilkinson (2012) Land grabbing and global capitalist accumulation: key features in Latin America. *Canadian Journal of Development Studies,* 33:402-416; Sun J, T Yu-xin, J Liu (2017) Telecoupled land-use changes in distant countries. *Journal of Integrative Agriculture,* 16(2):368-376.
13. Wallace RG and R Wallace (eds) (2016) *Neoliberal Ebola: Modeling Disease Emergence from Finance to Forest and Farm.* Springer Press: Chaim.
14. Xiao W and G Ziao (2018) Agricultural land and rural-urban migration in China: A new pattern. *Land Use Policy,* 74:142-150.
15. Koh D (2020) Migrant workers and COVID-19. *Occupational and Environmental Medicine,* 77(9): 634-636.
16. Ho V (2020) 'Everyone tested positive': Covid devastates agriculture workers in California's heartland. *The Guardian,* August 8. https://www.theguardian.com/us-news/2020/aug/08/california-covid-19-central-valley essential-workers.
17. Mora JM (2020) *Costa Rica's Covid-19 Response Scapegoats Nicaraguan Migrants.* NACLA, July 2020. https://nacla.org/news/2020/07/13/costa-rica-covid-nicaraguan-migrants.
18. McGrath S (2013) Fuelling global production networks with *slave labour?*: Migrant sugar cane workers in the Brazillian ethanol GPN. *Geoforum,* 44:32-43; Wallace R, LF Chaves, LR Bergmann, C Ayres, L Hogerwerf, R Kock, and RG Wallace (2018) *Clear-Cutting Disease Control: Capital-Led Deforestation, Public Health Austerity, and Vector-Borne Infection.* Springer, Cham.
19. Kremen C, A Iles, and C Bacon (2012) Diversified farming systems: An agroecological, systems-based alternative to modern industrial agriculture. *Ecology and Society,* 17(4):1-19.
20. Ewers RM, JPW Scharlemann, A Balmford and RE Green (2009) Do increases in agricultural yield spare land for nature? *Global Change Biology,* 15:1716-1726.
21. Angelsen A and D Kaimowitz (eds) (2001) *Agricultural Technologies and Tropical Deforestation.* Center for International Forestry Research CABI Publishing, New York.
22 . Perfecto I, J Vandermeer, and A Wright (2019). *Nature's Matrix: Linking Agriculture, Biodiversity Conservation and Food Sovereignty.* Routledge.
23. Wallace RG, A Liebman, D Weisberger, T Jonas, L Bergmann, R Kock, and R Wallace (2020) The origins of industrial agricultural pathogens. In RG Wallace, *Dead Epidemiologists: On the Origins of COVID-19.* Monthly Review Press, pp 102-129.
24. Liebman A and RG Wallace (2020) A factory farm fungus among us? In A Tsing, J Deger, A Keleman, F Zhou et al. (eds), *Feral Atlas: The More-Than-Human Anthropocene.* Stanford University Press, Stanford.
25. Wezel A, S Bellon, T Doré, C Francis, D Vallod, and C David (2009) Agroecology as a science, movement and a practice. *Agronomy for Sustainable Development,* 29: 503-515; Rosset PM and MA Altieri (2017) *Agroecology: Science and Politics.* Practical Action Publishing.
26. Perfecto I and J Vandermeer (2010) The agroecological matrix as alternative to the land-sparing/ agriculture intensification model. PNAS, 107(13): 5786-5791; Hecht SB and A Cockburn (2011) *The Fate of the Forest.* Chicago: University of Chicago Press.
27. Hecht SB and A Cockburn (2011) *The Fate of the Forest.* Chicago: University of Chicago Press.
28. Rosset, PM and ME Martínez-Torres (2012) Rural social movements and agroecology: context, theory, and process. *Ecology and Society,* 17(3):17; Anderson CR, J Bruil, MJ Chappell, et al. (2019)

From transition to domains of transformation: Getting to sustainable and just food systems through agroecology. *Sustainability,* 11(19):5272.

29. Wolfe P (2006) Settler colonialism and the elimination of the native. *Journal of Genocide Research,* 8(4):387-409; Zoomers A (2010) Globalization and the foreignization of space: seven processes driving the current global land grab; Fairbairn M (2020) *Fields of Gold: Financing the Global Land Rush.* Cornell University Press, Ithaca, NY.

30. Chappell MJ, H Wittman, CM Bacon et al. (2013) Food sovereignty: an alternative paradigm for poverty reduction and biodiversity conservation in Latin America. *F1000 Research,* 2:235

31. Chazdon RL, et al. (2009) The potential for species conservation in tropical secondary forests. *Conservation Biology,* 23:1406-1417.

32. Dalle SP and S de Blois (2006) Shorter fallow cycles affect the availability of noncrop plant resources in a shifting cultivation system. *Ecology and Society,* 11:2. http://www.ecologyandsociety.org/vol11/iss2/art2.

33. Coomes OT, Y Takasaki, and J Rhemtulla (2011) Land-use poverty traps identified in shifting cultivation systems shape long-term tropical forest cover. *PNAS,* 108 (34):13925-13930.

34. Zhu Y, H Chen, J Fan, et al. (2000) Genetic diversity and disease control in rice. Nature, 406:718-722.

35. Wallace RG, A Liebman, D Weisberger, T Jonas, L Bergmann, R Kock, and R Wallace (2020). The origins of industrial agricultural pathogens. In R Wallace, *Dead Epidemiologists: On the Origins of COVID-19.* Monthly Review Press, New York, pp 102-129.

36. Chaves LF, JE Calzada, C Rigg, A Valderrama, NL Gottdenker, and A Saldaña (2013) Leishmaniasis sand fly vector density reduction is less marked in destitute housing after insecticide thermal fogging. *Parasites & Vectors,* 6:164; Chaves LF (2018). The dialectics of malaria bednet use in Sub-Saharan Africa, In T Awerbuch, MS Clark, PJ Taylor, (eds.) *The Whole is the Truth: Essays in Honor of Richard Levins.* The Pumping Station, Arlington, MA, pp. 56-80; Chaves LF, M Ramírez Rojas, S Delgado Jiménez, M Prado, and R Marín Rodríguez (2020) Housing quality improvement is associated with malaria transmission reduction in Costa Rica. *Socio-Economic Planning Sciences,* 100951.